OH NO NO

by Christian Friend

To begin with may I greet you with are heart of thanks and gratitude that you have chosen to purchase this book. Clearly someone is a lot more open to talk on the subject of Jesus than I was myself only a few years hence.

My aim in what follows, I must be clear from the outset, is to share as transparently as is polite (the 'polite' means I won't be going into too much gory detail about my personal life) my experiences and my convictions regarding the person of Jesus, in terms of who he is and what this means for us all:

If you had caught me from the age I started thinking about such things, say 18-ish up until 2005, so the not too distant past, you would have found my assessment of Christian belief amounting to something like the following:

Christianity:

At best: A strict code necessary in times gone by, I guess, to bring us to this point of a structured society but now more or less irrelevant. Something previous generations in this country, due to their lack of education, in a harsh age, when coal was king and "life were grim", clung to like a crutch for comfort.

At worst: A dictatorial form of control, designed by men to suppress the masses.

Jesus:

At best: Probably a good man, a teacher, from a long time ago. Thankfully though now, we live in a more enlightened age than when people really believed that it was either his way or the highway. Christmas is alright though.

At worst: A fictitious construct of evil men seeking..... (see above)

Either way it was all a very long time ago.

Holy Spirit:

At best: God gas?

At worst: God gas?

God:

At best: Exists on an ethereal plain somewhere beyond our reach. Something that through a journey of learning and self-discovery we can learn to live in tune with, so to speak. Perhaps?

At worst: Some grey haired beardy old man looking disdainfully down upon us from a great distance, all Greek and Zeus like but having done away with his contingent of lesser Gods and of course obviously part of a dictatorial form of control.....

Every individual reading this will obviously have their own take on these topics. Yet I am counting on the fact that all of us will recognise some of these attitudes, if not as our own, then at least as the products, though not exclusive, of a pervading cultural attitude with regards to Christianity in the UK.('Christianity' meaning the teachings of Jesus in this instance) As far as I was concerned anyway, out of all the religious theories around, Christianity was the one that wasn't to be touched, even with the fabled excrement covered stick. I was open to just about anything else, to be honest, but this Jesus stuff was old news, I wasn't interested.

Because of the negative connotations outlined above, by the time I was a young adult even the very word "God" had been removed from my vocabulary as a serious means of describing the creator and sustainer of life.

(Notes Added posthumously) On reflection my stance was probably more extreme than I cared to admit here. At my Grandma's funeral when I was around 21 I recall refusing to shake the hand of the

minister who performed the modest service, as we departed, due to my firm conviction that he and others like him, with their "religion", were responsible for causing throughout history multitudes to unnecessarily experience the bereavement that we were now having to bare.

A few years down the line at the outset of my family, although I eventually relented, my feelings toward Christianity were so strong that I objected strongly to celebrating Christmas as a family.

Contents:

Encounters of a Holy Kind

Although it is by no means my intention to write an extensive biography, a few lines at this juncture I feel are necessary to give you a little of my own background, or in some cases my own view of our shared background, to reassure you that I didn't come in on the last flying saucer.

Although never taken to church or taught any religious doctrine, other than hymns sung in school assembly, growing up in Woodsetts, constantly surrounded by the fields, woods and streams, I don't recall ever thinking that God didn't exist, but religion was never part of home life. For example, if you had of asked me, at any point in the 20 years I lived there, what the inside of the village church looked like I wouldn't have been able to tell you. Additionally, the only biblical literature in our house was a St Michael's book of Bible stories that someone had obviously bought my mum at some point as a gift, which I viewed throughout the time I lived at home with complete disdain. The book was so untouched it is still in remarkably good condition to this day.

My only other encounters with faith could be counted on one hand. I remember clearly one occasion at about the age of 10 attempting to read parts of a Gideon Bible left in a hotel room, but finding the words colder a deader than any other book I had ever tried to read.

No, the bliss of my childhood I alluded to in the Introduction had no connection with organised religion or rigorous Sunday schooling, but more to do with football matches that were as though they were the event of the age, endless summers of mucking about in fields and down lanes, racing push-bikes and Mr Freeze ice-poles.

The schools in Woodsetts were heavenly places. If the weather was dry we were let loose on large, often freshly mowed playing fields. Once out there, each area of the playing fields was like a different world with its own atmosphere and experiences; whether it was

8

around the border, amongst the flowering elderberry bushes, or by the strangely positioned tall bushes that acted as a divider between upper and lower areas pictured below.

Generally, football was my priority although rolling down banks and playing army were also deemed equally worthwhile pursuits. The school was also full of such characters, everyone was very different yet equally fascinating and I recall admiring, to the point of envy almost, the talents and gifts of many. Friends and friendships were Spielberg-esque – as were the girls (I'm saying they were pretty, not that they looked like E.T!). The fact that friendships were formed there that have endured and the experiences we shared are remembered still is its own testimony really.

Secondary education was more difficult; from the village school to the school that was the size of a village. Fortunately a group of us were placed in a class together that formed the largest "tribe" and we survived more or less remaining friends when we left whilst acquiring some new ones on the way.

Young Adulthood

At school, as some may recall, art was my thing and following on from school, officially, my pursuit was to study Graphic Design.

However, following school, my passion for drawing was being eclipsed by a passion for music which became the driving force of my life and the main focus of my energies throughout my college years and beyond.

If you will allow me, I'll just explain a little bit about this as it has relevance to what follows. As we go on I promise I will be banging on about myself a lot less.

What was it that captured my whole being so much about music?

Well a combination of things. The fact that the music I was listening to was being performed by people who were part of the same demographic as me and, following a few wardrobe additions and a trip to the hairdressers, could pass as our older siblings was part of it to begin with. That a music could be "ours", belonging to one generation and not another, was important to me also as I was hoping, like most, to be markedly different to my parents. Whether this was from me or from the music is up for debate, but either way I bought into it. Obviously music had been around a lot more than religion growing up, and it was always something I liked, but never before had I connected with music like I did in my latter teen years, never had I gone to sleep with headphones on lost in sound. Never had songs understood my heartaches, loves and losses or given me aspirations and direction in terms of my attitude towards life. Music quickly became my identity and I picked up a guitar for the first time at around 17. My paternal father played so I progressed quicker, and had more support than my peers who began playing at the same time.

Following the initial burst of enthusiasm, the thing that spurred me on to dedicate so much time and effort to this pursuit was, what I deemed as, the power of music to evoke feelings within, or to paint pictures of feelings that could be experienced by the listener, that made it more alive and a much more exciting prospect creatively than static art. Over the next few years, an expanding horizon of musical styles, combined with drink and drugs, made it appear as though, through music, you could be transported anywhere and do anything. Social change, spiritual awakening, you name it.

And if my music had the potential to transport people places, where was it I wanted to take people?

Where did I want to go?

I can't be sure when I first accepted it to be the case, but as we reached employment age it became of grave concern to me that our "bliss" that had been leaking steadily was on its dregs and a strange and unwelcome change was upon my world.

Where did I want to go?

Back!

I didn't want to be small again and run around in football kits and tracksuits, you must understand, but clearly something had been lost on the way between 8 and 20 that ought not to have been lost. Why must we follow on generation after generation becoming older and colder? Weren't we different? Surely there was a way to hold on to the vibrancy and innocence of childhood, and if there was then maybe I could put it in a piece of music or a song, the way it appeared musicians I was listening to at the time had!

At the point this idea formulated music became more than a passion but a religion and my self- assigned purpose in life!

So I embarked on full-time study: Life and Music, with the minor annoyance of a qualification in Graphic Design. A Beatles-inspired love of eastern philosophy, encouraged by my paternal father who read extensively and taught on the subject voluntarily, soon found me meditating regularly. Ancient Hindu writings like the Bhagavad Gita, plus the Islamic musings of Kalil Gibran, the esoteric adventure stories of Richard Bach, and the teachings of Krishnamurti (If you're not familiar with these people then they are on YouTube) were, I thought, opening my eyes to a different way that appeared to hold the answers to all my burning questions which by now, after reading up on various modern history topics, encompassed concerns about the cause of human suffering. By the second year of my Graphic Design course I was attending philosophy night classes studying Plato, Socrates and stuff like that.

I was unravelling my habitual thinking, I was analysing and getting to the root of my fears, I was quietening my mind and staying awake and alert with regards to the chattering of my subconscious. I was journeying inward to find the life within! Spiritually evolving myself through meditation and study back to my roots and my bliss, fixing the world one soul at a time, starting with the man in the mirror. To live was to learn and to grow, and it was about as far away from draconian Christianity as you could get and very pleased with it all I was too.

By 22, I was committed to doing music full-time, no more Graphic Design holding me back, living at my Dad's and working part-time in a couple of pubs.

Returning to his house following a lunch-time shift one day during the spring of 1999, I was approached not far from my destination by two nervous looking young American lads. Mormons, about my own age, one of whom I perceived was particularly insecure, probably owing to his acne and red hair. Obviously, spiritually evolved and learned as I was, I was more than willing to debate with them on the subject of the nature of God.

I don't remember the structure of the conversation, but at some point the more confident of the pair pulls out a leaflet which at the bottom has a black and white picture of a man kneeling in prayer in woods with a heavenly light falling on his upraised head. As the missionary held the leaflet, he recounted to me the testimony of how the Church's pioneer, Joseph Smith, perplexed by the arguments and counter arguments of various Christian denominations, prayed, sought and spoke with God at age 14 for an answer to the question of which of the local warring Churches he should throw his lot in with.

As he is speaking though, I become, steadily at first, and then completely overwhelmed by this euphoric presence like nothing else I have experienced. My focus becomes fixed on the image that is angled towards me, which becomes alive to the point that I feel I am there in the wood with the kneeling figure. I am literally engulfed and laid bare, yet I try, as I am able, to withhold this from the pair and maintain my composure. The missionary finishes his reading and I am able to scramble back to my non-euphoric state.

Although there was undeniably more to what the missionary was telling me than just a wacky story, not for the last time my pride overcame my heart and I simply took the literature from them and fled.

As the moments, minutes, hours, days pass I rationalise the encounter. I decide that I am mistrustful of the use of imagery, perhaps it was some kind of hypnosis? Anyway, I am not joining some Waco style cult and moreover I am more than happy to continue along the path I had set for myself. Plus I have a demo to finish.

I put the whole episode behind me and continue with my music and eastern philosophy.

After a couple of years at my Dad's, inevitably, we agree to disagree over various matters that I don't remember anymore and part company. Fortunately by now I have joined a band and I move to Leeds to live a student life with them. Supporting myself by working full-time now in a city centre pub, ever progressing, in a spiritual sense, along the road of rough experience and enlightenment, my beliefs are now infused into my music as I zealously take on the role of leader and singer in the new band.

It's 2001 and while searching for a locally advertised reggae festival myself and a fellow band member mistakenly identify a church tent meeting on the outskirts of Chapeltown as our destination. The sounds we hear coming out of the tent, although not reggae, are of interest nevertheless as the harmonies of a Gospel Choir drift our way. Drawing closer, we are approached by two little old Caribbean ladies who we hope can possibly provide directions. Following the initial polite greetings the conversation turns to matters of belief, namely, whether we have any or not. Buoyed by the approval of my new peers and my zeal for my self-assigned musical/spiritual purpose, I am happy to take the lead in the conversation and make it known to our new acquaintances that they are in the presence of enlightened individuals.

Standing about forty meters from the entrance of the marquee, which is off to the right, I explain to the two ladies my acceptance of their faith, but also the superiority of my own learning, as I share with them Gandhi's 'all roads lead to God' teaching of how different religions are like different sides of the same spiritual mountain. "That's not what Jesus said," one of the ladies began... The response I received from then on would, in different circumstances, have provoked a rapid counter response had it not been that from that precise moment onward a sudden rush of the same euphoria again began to flood my whole being. "He said I am the way the truth and the life no man comes unto the father except through me" she went on to say and expound upon as all the while, which seemed like an age, my senses were overwhelmed.

The world around me came alive like never before with the presence that engulfed my being, as if prior to this I had been viewing the world only in 2D. My eyes lifted towards the dramatic dusk sky that was the painted backdrop to the marquee and the city, yet insurmountably greater. The presence that was all about me and engulfed me had a message. (Not that audible words were heard as such, but it was more the sense that if you awoke one morning and opened your eyes expecting to see the familiar four walls, yet were confronted with the inside of Buckingham palace and the Queen stood before you, you would be aware that one: you are dressed inappropriately and two: you might have missed something in your diary.) What I was aware of in my encounter was that God knew me and had always known me and that I, on some level knew him, but not like I had at one time in my life. The reason for my not knowing him was not him having abandoned me to my own devices that I should be searching high and low for him, but rather that it was I who had rejected him.

My eyes came down from the sky; the Christian witness had finished her reply and invited us to the service that was taking place in the tent. The presence still engulfed my whole being. I looked at the light filled entrance to the meeting and it was as though it was the very entrance to heaven: I was aware that it was my home and the will of God for me enter in.

Were they aware of all that was happening to me? If they were, they didn't show it. Was Paul, my new found friend and band-mate, able to detect any change in me? I wanted to fall to my knees, weep and go in, but what I felt impelled to do was definitely not the actions of the person I had led him to believe I was!

I had always been quietly self-conscious and this, seasoned with pride, found me again scrambling for normality . Against the cry of my whole being, I declined the offer and returned to the car parked a short distance away. Walking away with the tent at our backs, I ought to still have turned and run back but I didn't. As we drove away, a dark empty fear gripped me this time unlike before. We found the reggae festival but I couldn't be there, the terrible nameless anxiety that now gripped me was even more intense. This was not where I was meant to be! I got Paul to drive me home.

The fear that gripped me faded when I returned home but the

conviction of what I had encountered and the decision I had made remained. Impelled by my own conscience I needed to do something. I needed to do what I hadn't done when I had been called. I had searched for God all this time, spent hours, days, mediating, years of study hoping to understand how to break through the veil of life and ascend to some ethereal dimension.

Now I get all that, but not of my own effort, but after some little old Caribbean woman quoting words from the Bible! That was not what I was expecting! Neither was it what I wanted.

Nevertheless, I had received what I had searched for. Once I could count as a blip, an anomaly, but after this it was now undeniably incumbent upon me to do something about these experiences. What exactly that "something" was I had no idea, but as a start I decided to return the next day alone to see if the tent was still there.

Not knowing which bus to catch to that part of Leeds but knowing the route we had taken by car, I set out from town on foot to find the tent. I don't tell anyone about it obviously, what would I say? God spoke to me and I walked away but I need to go back! No. Best to keep that to myself I think, for now at least.

Just leaving the safety of the centre of Leeds, whilst refereeing the raging arguments within, for and against the validity of the exercise, a taste of the dark empty fear I experienced returns and puts me on edge. I become aware of a couple of dodgy lads on the other side of the road. One I notice gestures covertly in my direction, they walk off in the opposite direction, but two minutes down the road I notice they are following behind at a distance and thirty seconds later they are closer. I leg it away from my pursuers and also the location of the tent. If I were that way inclined, I would have thought something didn't want me to return to that place?

The next day I try again and succeed. It is the middle of the day and the tent is empty apart from a man giving an informal talk to a small group, so I listen from a distance. He's a Reverend but quite young and he begins to tell us in a very disarming, comical fashion about a long standing friend he has who didn't believe in God but with whom he would share his faith with. This friend was going on holiday to Turkey, so the Reverend suggested some biblical sites there that he might want to check out. On his return, the Reverend recounted to us how his friend testified to having been in one of these places when this euphoric feeling came upon him! The group start to laugh knowingly, the way only Caribbean people can, as the Reverend encouraged his listeners to continue to pray for their friends as 'You never know when the Holy Spirit is going to show up!'.

Is that what it was then!?

The Holy Spirit?

What does that mean?

The talk was over, I was greeted and handed a program which contained a schedule for the rest of the meetings which I found out were organised by a local church and there was an address.

Over the days that became weeks, that became months, that became years that followed, the sense that there was something required of me never went away. I continued purposefully with music, hoping that it would after all repay me for the time I had invested in it and maybe provide for the young family I had acquired by now. I visited the church that organised the tent meetings on occasion and heard some good things and also other things that I really couldn't stomach. At the end of the services there they bowed their heads in prayer and asked if anyone in the congregation would like to come to the Alter and accept Jesus as their personal saviour. Was this what I needed to do? I really didn't want to stand up there in-front of all those people. If I ever stopped long enough in the service to hear the Alter call I stayed put.

As time went on, it became increasingly obvious that my self-assigned purpose in life of enlightening the world through music wasn't turning out as I'd hoped or planned. Neither, for that matter, was my personal life. Now I don't want to go in to gory details here, but by 2004 we had reached critical mass. It was decision time and I had made my decision that would undoubtedly affect my whole life from that point on. I just had one thing which I still had to do, just to put it finally to rest...

I would go to the church and see if God had anything more to say to me at this critical hour. I didn't expect he would, or if he did I expected he would no doubt agree that I was doing the right thing.

I turned up late; much of the service was over, just the sermon to listen to. Again I don't recall a great deal of the content until the Alter call when the pastor told us not to allow our current situation to prevent us from coming to the Alter even if it was...

He continued to describe my exact circumstances! There was a call in my heart which I for once decided, in the name of experience you must understand, to heed. I walked to the front of the church with an attitude of 'okay let's see what happens'. Was the presence going to flood my soul again? Perhaps this time it would be even stronger? Perhaps I would be knocked to the floor? The Pastor prayed, I repeated his prayer which included a request for guidance, whilst maintaining my awareness against any sly tricks they might employ.

No tricks, no collapsing either, and I was handed some literature in the back of the church, told I had been saved by grace, my 'sins' were forgiven and church was over.

Although initially slightly disappointed at the lack of fireworks, as I stepped out into the world and engaged again with life I quickly became aware that something was fundamentally different within me. Something had undeniably changed inside, a presence now accompanied me, through the following hours, days and weeks, guiding me away from my previous plan of action and through unravelling the mess I had created in the preceding years.At times I would wrestle with this guidance and try again to chart the Bible. The once cold dead words of this book now jumped of the page like hot coals lighting fires in my heart. Jesus, it appeared, was real.

As a proponent of anti-Christian philosophies, my road to fully fledged faith from here was, to my shame, more of a slow begrudging acceptance and confession of a truth that I was uncomfortable with, rather than a bold changing of the flag. Even once accepting Jesus as my saviour, yet again, it was another year until I committed myself to attending one church full-time and seeking guidance to help me overcome my continuing misgivings about the teachings of the faith.

You might be asking the question at this juncture what it is that I think is so special about me that I assume to have received such revelation. Well, historically, with many cases (and particularly in mine), I think it is more the case of "if God can do it for one as rebellious, wrapped up and full of all manner of deceit as I was, then he can do it for anyone". To give you a measure of the gravity of my situation, although I was unconcerned about such things as right or wrong actions at the time, life equals experience equals growth was my philosophy, in my Jack Kerouac *On The Road* lifestyle – minus the road – and you could, before the second witness of the Holy Spirit, have counted me in for all of the Ten Commandments. By the time I got to church it was a lot worse. The result of this was that, despite all by best efforts and even though I was in no way entangled by the guilt and shame of my actions, to give it the right name now, my joy was all gone. By even the very lowest standards the blessings I received and have continued to receive are by nobody's standards deserved.

In what follows I will share the painfully acquired understanding that helped me to overcome many of my previously held misgivings with regards to the teaching of Jesus and the Bible. The first and foremost obstacle, however, for anyone approaching the teachings of Jesus is the question of who he is.

Any answer I alone might provide to this question will more than likely fall short of the mark, as it ought to, because there is a biblical principle that needs to be adhered to here. This principle was at work in the ministry of Jesus and in the encounters I described previously. The principle being that a testimony is only valid if it is witnessed by two persons or, in other words: if we are to accept anything there must be evidence from at least two sources. On its own my testimony, I am aware, is not enough to convince anyone of its truth, however I pray that whilst reading it the Holy Spirit that convicted me will do the same work in all those who read it.

Otherwise, my hope is not that from my reading testimony anyone would be led to make an intellectual decision to follow the teachings of Jesus, but that hopefully you would be charitable enough to accept my testimony is not a lie or a delusion and that this would in turn encourage you to open the door of your heart wide enough to allow in, even just the possibility, that there may be something more to Jesus that you previously thought and that this might be something worth seeking out for yourself.

Jesus taught his followers:

Matthew 6:33
New International Version (NIV)

But seek first his kingdom and his righteousness, and all these things will be given to you as well.

Why is finding out who Jesus is such a big deal?

Well unless we have lived under a rock our whole lives, we at some level know that what is proposed in Jesus is the answer to the most pressing questions of life:

What are we doing here?

What is our purpose?

Where are we heading?

If it is possible to hear from God himself on these subjects, then the way we view various attempts to answer these questions understandably is irrevocably changed forever.

A bit of theology:

Far from this hearing from God stuff being a strange or new idea, what we are actually talking about here is the very foundation of the Christian teaching that is also the foundation of much of the societies of the western world. That in Jesus you can know! You can know for a certainty that God is real and you can know unequivocally that Jesus is the Son of God!

Listen here to what Jesus himself taught.

Matthew 16: 16-18
New International Version (NIV)

'Who do you say that I am?' Simon Peter answered, 'You are the Christ, the Son of the living God' Jesus replied 'Blessed are you Simon son of Jonah, for this was not revealed to you by man, but by my Father in heaven. And I tell you that on this rock I will build my church, and the gates of Hades will not overcome it.'

John 1: 18
New International Version (NIV)

No one has ever seen God, but the one and only Son, who is himself God and is in closest relationship with the Father, has made him known.

The meaning of this I hope is clear, within the context of what we are talking about: the church or in the Greek ecclesia (called out) people's foundation, that shall not be overcome, is a revelation of who Jesus is, direct from God. The current incumbent of the position of Jesus within the earth is the Holy Spirit, sometimes referred to as the advocate, who witnesses to us of this truth.

John 15: 26
New International Version (NIV)

"When the Advocate comes, whom I will send to you from the Father—the Spirit of truth who goes out from the Father—he will testify about me".

Surely then the natural question is: if we can know then how do we go about it?

Well not only does He speak, but He is also able and willing to reveal Himself personally to anyone who might be audacious enough to seek Him. Occasionally, as God is in no ways bound, He'll also reveal himself and speak to those who aren't particularly looking for Him too. It is important to understand that although we may seek him and it is right to do so, it is not us that somehow forcibly break into His presence through our own effort. Rather that we, out of the longings in the depths of our heart, begin to call out to Him, it is then He who hears and arranges the time and place where He will reveal to us the light and glory of His presence. It is God that does the revealing at his discretion, rather than we who force His hand, thus nobody can boast or claim superiority of having attained any blessing through endeavour.

John 6: 44
New International Version (NIV)

"No one can come to me unless the Father who sent me draws him, and I will raise him up at the last day.

1 Corinthians 1: 28-31
New International Version (NIV)

God chose the lowly things of this world and the despised things—
and the things that are not—to nullify the things that are, so that
no one may boast before him. It is because of him that you are in
Christ Jesus, who has become for us wisdom from God—that is,
our righteousness, holiness and redemption. Therefore, as it is
written: "Let the one who boasts boast in the Lord."

The Bible tells us that when we are not in relationship with Him,
God is jealous for our attention and our affections, because we are
His creation. Also He wants you to be in no doubt as to whom it is
who calls you.

Jesus said:

Matthew 7: 7-8
Amplified Bible (AMP)

"Keep on asking and it will be given you; keep on seeking and you
will find; keep on knocking [reverently] and [the door] will be
opened to you.

For everyone who keeps on asking receives; and he who keeps on
seeking finds; and to him who keeps on knocking, [the door] will
be opened."

There is no set process other than the scripture above that we can
follow, nor any preparatory steps we can take to ensure we are
ready for the response. He is available to everyone, however it is
said He is a gentlemen and will not enter in where He is not
welcome, as in William Holborn-Hunt's painting, *Light of the World*,
where a cloaked Jesus holding a lantern stands at a bedraggled
doorway; He stands at the door, as He always has, patiently
awaiting your invitation that He may bring his light to where you
are.

If you have experienced His presence at all prior to now, then I would encourage you to be bolder than your friend and speak plainly the desire of your heart in sincere prayer, inviting Jesus to reveal Himself to you personally.

In faithfulness to His word, you will receive your revelation. There are no two the same, so it is impossible to advise you of what to expect, but do expect. It's a 'different strokes for different folks' kind of thing. It may knock you off your feet or it may simply be a quiet undeniable word spoken in your ear, but it will come and it will be undeniably from God.

For any whom, I hope, have made it this far, but who still have difficulty with all of this for one reason or another – maybe you have had a strongly atheist upbringing or you have had bad experiences with people who claimed to be Christian yet have treated you in a deeply un-Christian way and now even the suggestion that there is anything virtuous to be found in Jesus has become offensive to you – I would ask you to consider the following.

For those who have had bad experiences, I would ask you to study the life of Christ, to see if you find anything untoward in his behaviour or his actions. Because it is Him I am proposing, not any 'Christian' organisation or anyone else. From my own brief journey it is clear that many organisations that claim to be Christian have a very woolly definition of what that actually means, yet the Bible, in contrast, is very clear. We will go into this more in further chapters. Put simply, Jesus said a tree is known by its fruit so don't let any individuals actions keep you from seeking him.

For the atheist, I would ask you to consider that for someone to state that an all knowing, all intelligent being who stands outside of the realms of time categorically does not exist, they would have to be all knowing and standing outside of the realms of time themselves. But as human beings have a limited life span, and therefore our knowledge and experience is also limited, we cannot fully know all things. It follows then that it is possible that some may experience things that others do not. If you accept this then you are not an atheist but an agnostic; you are saying that as far as you know there appears to be no evidence of any kind of superior intelligence at work.

From there I would ask you to consider what Psalm 19 says:

Psalm 19: 1-6
New International Version (NIV)

The heavens declare the glory of God;
The skies proclaim the work of his hands;
Day after day they pour forth speech;
Night after night they display knowledge;
There is no speech or language where their voice is not heard;
Their voice goes out into all the earth, their words to the end of the world;

We have heard all the scientific theories about how the world came into being, but we need to have a tender heart to see the world in this way and ask: If it's all merely accidental then why is the world so beautiful? Why all the colours and countless varieties? Why is it, amongst many other things, that when there is a total eclipse, that the moon is exactly the right size to hide the sun. Why is it that babies being born only take their first gasps of air when they are completely out and not when their heads first appear? Surely these simple facts are enough for us to be open to the idea that there may be a designer behind all of this.

Yet note this from the preceding scripture that although "*The heavens declare the glory of God;* and *The skies proclaim the work of his hands*" it does not read that the heavens contain the glory of God and the skies are where God is. The Bible is clear that the natural world is God's handiwork yet it does not assert that he is to be found in it physically or somehow through it spiritually. This world view is known as Naturalism, yet so often a naturalist argument is accepted without question as cause to discredit the supernatural message of Jesus.

Yet, with regards to Naturalism, to accept the earth to be merely an accidental occurance, scientists are agreed, is improbable to say the least, lest that there should be billions upon billions of other universes and we just happen to be the fluke one. (For sticklers for detail this is the multi-verse theory of which Stephen Hawking is a proponent).

Ironically, to accept such a theory would truly require that most derided of attributes, 'blind faith', as it is never going to be proven or disproven this side of the next millennium. Others would have you believe that, although the world may appear designed, because we cannot observe God through standard scientific techniques, we cannot entertain any of this which is a bit like saying "because I don't know how to play a musical instrument I don't believe music exists". The other aspect of this argument is that if we could somehow physically observe God as some molecule or bacteria, as part of physical creation, then this would be in direct contradiction to the Bible which tells us that God is invisible:

Colossians 1: 15
New International Version (NIV)

The Son is the image of the invisible God, the firstborn over all creation.

What do we suppose, also, would be the reaction of the scientific world if they discovered God in a Petri-dish or under a microscope? Would Man then suddenly begin to proclaim the wonders of God?

I doubt this very much. More than likely such a discovery would become the ultimate triumph of Man over God! Man the Lord of the world on high observing his redundant creator at work under Man's observation!

Certainly the recent popularisation of aggressively anti-Christian philosophies have made it more apparent than ever that when it comes to the teachings of Jesus there is no sitting on the fence.

Luke 12: 53
New International Version (NIV)

They will be divided, father against son and son against father, mother against daughter and daughter against mother, mother-in-law against daughter-in-law and daughter-in-law against mother-in-law.

God has not chosen to reveal himself through a Petri dish or under a microscope but through his son, the truth of which the person of the Holy Spirit bears witness to in our time. An encounter with Jesus is the difference between the son and his father and the mother and her daughter in the scripture above and the first question of this book is one that each of us has to answer. I have included quotes from the Bible that clearly state who He would have us believe He is and how we should prove Him. Are we prepared to try Jesus?

In the course of this book we are going to be asking many questions, the answers to which are no doubt going to require more than just words on a page to accept. Certainly Jesus, The Son who is the image of the invisible God, wasn't merely a wise man. The Bible contains the records of outlandish statements He made about himself, and about His work in the world that, if proven false, as C. S. Lewis rightly points out, ought to be disregarded as the ravings of a mad man but, if found to be true, and once we fully understand them, warrant maybe more than we could ever give in one lifetime.

Six years after being drawn to the other side of the fence myself I still have much to learn, but also much to give Him thanks for. So many trials, toils and snares He has brought me through that my overwhelming desire now is to be of service to Him whose faithfulness and love have exceeded not only my expectations but also anything I could ever have possibly imagined. I hope what follows will in some measure be that.

Adam and Eve: You Don't Expect Me to Believe That!

Perhaps the most common reasons we are likely to disregard Christianity in this generation, and something that was pretty high on my own list of objections, is what is commonly perceived, in light of scientific advances, as a lack of credibility in the biblical account of Creation. Unless we have had Christian apologists for parents, it's more than likely that before we approach adulthood, with the help of Secondary education, the big bang and evolution are so deeply embedded into all our thinking about the world around us, as the great and virtuous revelations of knowledge and truth they purport to be, that we are in no ways inclined to give credence to what we generally see as the previous age's dogmatic thinking on the subject of our origins. What reason, if any, would there be that would cause us to seriously consider any teaching that predates this intellectual breakthrough of our age?

Consequently, disregard, or in my case something more like contempt, for the biblical version of creation, more often than not, leads on to disregard for the Bible as a whole. 'If the beginning is a lie then why bother with the rest!' (There is a spiritual principle at work here which we will address maybe later.)

If we recognise ourselves as being subject to this scenario yet, by ways of revelation or inkling, have reason to believe that Jesus is more than just a story, then we might find relief in the fact that an immediate signed confession of our belief in the biblical account of the origins of the world and Man is not going to be required of us. If we're going to get something from this chapter though we will have to be able to suppress the knee-jerk dismissal of the Bible's take on this topic as we look into some of the lessons that are found within these much derided passages, that I have been surprised to discover as some of the most profound, awe inspiring and life affirming in the good book.

To cover every facet of this teaching would warrant several books by itself, so we shall inevitably fall short to some degree, but we shall try and focus on three fundamental questions that the Creation narrative in particular offers us answers to. These are: Who are we? Where are we at? And where are we heading?

Who are we?

Primarily the Bible is a spiritual book or, a book for the soul, if we are more comfortable with that term. It is also, factual, historical, prophetic and practical, but primarily spiritual or soul centred.

Ok, I understand we have to tread carefully and not make assumptions as some, as strange as it seems to me, may question even the very existence of the soul or spirit of a person.

To that I would ask the question: have we ever attended the funeral of a loved one of the sort where their body is on view? Although personally I find the practise rather macabre, the cold expressionless husk that bears no resemblance to the person you once knew, does serve as an undeniable testimony for the soul. As clear as day we are faced with the reality that the very essence of who that person was has clearly departed some time ago and what you are left staring at is only the vessel that the person you knew inhabited for a time.

Rather than being something morbid, is there not, on reflection, hope in this? Hope that there is more to people than just flesh and blood?

Even if we perhaps haven't had this experience, do we not get a sense of eternity when the face in the mirror changes over time whilst something within remains ever the same? This consistent personality within that departs at death is, in Bible terms, who we truly are and the part of us that will endure beyond death; our soul or spirit.

Moving on...

Genesis 1: 1-5
New International Version (NIV)

In the beginning God created the heavens and the earth. Now the earth was formless and empty, darkness was over the surface of the deep, and the Spirit of God was hovering over the waters.

And God said, "Let there be light," and there was light. God saw that the light was good, and he separated the light from the darkness. God called the light "day," and the darkness he called "night." And there was evening, and there was morning—the first day.

The rather obvious first lesson of Creation on the subject of 'Who are we?' is that we are created by God who is our father. This father of ours is also the same being that created the whole visible world. As we mentioned at the start, most of us are aware of the many scientific criticisms of this renowned passage of scripture; nevertheless science does not however find this 4000+ year old book to be in error with regards to the order in which life appears on the earth.

Concerning ourselves primarily with the spiritual message of Creation though, let us just gleam from the seven day account of Creation that the formation of our entire physical reality was "all in a week's work" for God and not a particularly burdensome task. Taking note also of the method of construction, 'And God said... and God said...',let's move on to the more personal aspects of what Creation actually says about us and our role and purpose in the earth.

I must admit that growing up having, to my recollection, never read Genesis I was convinced that the story of Adam and Eve was all about sex and how we shouldn't be doing it and how a man was punished for having sex with Eve. (An amazing feat of ignorance on my part)

This misconception crystallized and became such a part of my anti-Christian outlook on life, that I recall enthusing to friends over the Beatles film, Yellow Submarine, with reference to this subject. I would explain how, symbolically, these tall animated characters in the film that wore top hats and went around turning people grey by bonking them on the head with an apple represented this controlling belief system that had us under its spell by telling us that our most natural desires were wrong. The greyness represented the misery of becoming filled full of shame and self loathing that emanated from believing the lie of this constricting religion. All we needed to do, I would expound, was to shake off these ideas by mentally un-wrapping the mechanism of them, thus exposing the fallacy of what this draconian religion had managed to sneak into our subconscious, and we would be free!

Thankfully I stopped smoking drugs; it clearly wasn't doing me or my friends any favours! Also, thankfully this is not what Genesis says at all. In fact, sex is not even part of it.

What Genesis actually tells us, in a nutshell, is:

The first people that God created, Adam and Eve (remember, for the evolutionists, we are talking spiritually), from whom according to the narrative we inherit many of our own behavioural traits, were provided for in every way by God. They had a place to live, work to do, every fruit bearing plant for food and they were in frequent communication with their creator.

In this garden paradise were two special trees. One, the Tree of the Knowledge of Good and Evil, that Adam and Eve were warned by God not to harvest as it would result in their death; the second, the Tree of Life, would grant them eternal life by eating of its fruit. More than likely you know the story or you have an idea of the way it goes... Adam and Eve, with encouragement from a slippery acquaintance, go and do the very thing they were told not to, and then the proverbial poop hits the fan for humanity from that time on.

If we can manage to get beyond the knee-jerk dismissal and I manage to stay in my seat in church long enough to seriously consider the message of this scripture, then the foremost philosophical question/criticism of this scenario is often: 'Why on earth did God put the Tree of the Knowledge of Good and Evil there in the first place?' Surely this was God's first mistake or otherwise a cruel burden to place upon the innocent pair?

The answer to this particular riddle is an important one because it is one of the foundations of Christian teaching, but we will have to delve a little deeper into the text to find it. To this end then let us now consider an alternative scenario:

Metaphorically speaking, if within the Garden it were only possible for Adam and Eve (who are representative of humanity) to do those things that were within God's will then wouldn't they have simply been unwittingly subservient to God? And as such, merely highly advanced biochemical robots? Or, as I myself once believed, that if God somehow was the author of all our actions, whether good or bad, and they all simply became part of a limitlessly flexible one way journey toward God, then is not the result the same? Mankind ultimately has no choice with regards to how he lives out his days.

The Tree of Knowledge of Good and Evil in this scenario then represents the great gift of liberty afforded to humanity, specifically with regards to rejecting God as their role model should they so choose. The relationship that God attributes between himself and Adam and Eve further emphasises this point in that Adam and Eve are referred to not as God's servants, but as His children. It is only natural that a father should grant to his children, us, the right to determine our own course.

This 'liberty' of mankind that these scriptures speak of is one major factor in what makes the humanity of the Bible unique in all of

Creation. Attributed to us in these verses also is unparalleled power, unparalleled authority over the rest of Creation and a relationship and connection to God that makes humanity of utmost importance to Him. These differences are evidenced in the account of our formation where we are told that, as opposed to the rest of Creation, God, apparently, created us in His own likeness! Not that we grow up to be old, grey and beardy, but that as God is spirit, so we truly are also spirit.

John 4: 24
New International Version (NIV)

God is spirit, and his worshipers must worship in the Spirit and in truth.

Genesis 1: 26-27
New International Version (NIV)

Then God said, "Let us make mankind in our image, in our likeness, so that they may rule over the fish in the sea and the birds in the sky, over the livestock and all the wild animals, and over all the creatures that move along the ground."

So God created mankind in his own image,
in the image of God he created them;
male and female he created them.

Genesis 2: 7
New International Version (NIV)

Then the LORD God formed a man from the dust of the ground and breathed into his nostrils the breath of life, and the man became a living being.

Of note is the change of method from 'And God said this and it was, and God said that and it was...' to 'Come let us make...' Clearly a more focused effort was made with this project involving input from several personalities. The time invested in this project also denotes special importance, as following the five and half days required for creating everything in existence, from galaxies all the way down to insects with a day and a half to create every other living creature, half a day is set aside for the creation of a single man and woman. The chronology is not to be overlooked either, as it speaks again of the plan and position God has in mind for mankind, the implicit message being that Creation was prepared beforehand for us by our Father.

On completing His work, our Father takes time out to stand back and assess his work. We and all Creation are sealed with the approval of God who declares that we are "very good".

In the biblical scheme of things, the Kingdom of Heaven is obviously a monarchy where God reigns, but the earth however is where Man was given authority and freedom to reign, which means real choice and real independence! Far from being a few billion insignificant ants crawling on an accidentally foliaged rock in outer space, the Bible tells us that we are the sons and daughters of its creator, and our rightful position is to reign as such, living in communion with Him whilst executing our duties as the stewards of His world, His royal representatives on the earth.

I am about to state the obvious, I know, but our parents are our forerunners and not our creators; left without hindrance then, is it not only natural that we should seek to discover our true source?

If the God of the Bible is that source then it would mean that, as a result of us being "made in his image", we are selling ourselves extremely short by believing that we are no more than children of primordial soup. It would mean, among other things, that our words like His are creatively powerful, as can be our deeds; it means that we, like our Father, are eternal and that what we can aspire to become in this life is a lot more than we may have previously thought. "Who we are", individually, is only really going to be understood when we begin to understand His character and his specific purpose for our lives.

Where are we at?

I don't imagine that many of us will have much difficulty accepting the message of the first section of this chapter. I fear that won't remain true for what follows, as the acceptance of the lessons found within what is known as "the fall of man" are pivotal to everything that follows and, ironically, a stumbling stone for most. It is here that we need to be brave enough to be honest with ourselves and deeply sincere in our self enquiry if we are to ultimately benefit from the message of these explosive and famously misrepresented passages.

With the immense power conferred upon biblical Man, comes immense responsibility and immense consequences should this power be misused. As keepers of the world, Adam and Eve were categorically instructed as to what the result of going against their Father's instruction would bring.

Returning to the narrative, Adam and Eve are given a "garden of delight" in which to live, that supplies all their needs. Into this garden one day arrives a visitor we are told, who engages Eve in conversation.

Genesis 3: 1-6
New International Version (NIV)

Now the serpent was more crafty than any of the wild animals the LORD God had made. He said to the woman, "Did God really say, 'You must not eat from any tree in the garden'?" The woman said to the serpent, "We may eat fruit from the trees in the garden, but God did say, 'You must not eat fruit from the tree that is in the middle of the garden, and you must not touch it, or you will die.'" "You will not certainly die," the serpent said to the woman. "For God knows that when you eat from it your eyes will be opened, and you will be like God, knowing good and evil." When the woman saw that the fruit of the tree was good for food and pleasing to the eye, and also desirable for gaining wisdom, she took some and ate it. She also gave some to her husband, who was with her, and he ate it.

Now for those who are not prepared to accept the notion of a devil, then please persist – we will get on to that. For the time being it will suffice us to accept the idea that as well as granting freedom and liberty to mankind, to choose whether or not to do His will, God also granted the same privilege to a host of heavenly spiritual beings, one of whom, we are told in Ezekiel 28, turned against God taking many with him. This ultimate embodiment of cunning and deceitfulness, in this case, in the form of a serpent, whose deathly poison comes from his mouth (in contrast to God from whose mouth brings forth life) engages Eve, the younger of the two and therefore the one with least experience of God, in conversation.

Another name for the devil in the Bible is "The Accuser", and the first statement of the conversation made to Eve is an indirect or cloaked accusation aimed at God, "did God really say you could not eat of any of the fruit of the Garden?" This character obviously has a high opinion of himself, passing himself off as someone in a position to comment on God's integrity! In doing so he subtly promotes himself as an alternative authority to God. Eve immediately accepts the implied presuppositions and jumps to the defence of the accusation aimed at her creator, when a more appropriate response would have been to discipline the creature for his offence. The consequence of this is that she becomes embroiled in conversation with the enemy of her soul who proceeds to outwit her at every turn.

The serpent then adds to the earlier aspersions aimed at God by plainly describing God as a liar and a deceiver 'you shall not surely die' he says and proceeds to attack the first of the three main weaknesses of mankind outlined in the Bible, our Pride, by suggesting to Eve that if she were to go against God's will she would become as God! Up to this point Adam and Eve were living, trusting that what God says was right was right and what God says was wrong was wrong and behaving accordingly. The name of the tree speaks of the opportunity it represents to decide for themselves what to call right and what to call wrong; in essence, to be their own law maker instead of taking God's word for it.

Secondly, exploiting the lust of the eyes, mankind's second weakness, he shows her the fruit. Its attractive appearance adds to the allure of the idea that eating the fruit might be of benefit to her.

Then thirdly, she indulges the lust of her physical frame and finds that this fruit is satisfying to her stomach too. I tended to think of this as a sleeping beauty moment where she takes one bite and falls to the ground, but the Bible says simply that she ate it, which would suggest that she consumed the whole thing. Adam comes over, hears all the same stuff and drinks it all in just as Eve did.

To de-religiousify (my own word) this, might help make this situation clearer for some:

The New Testament tells us that God is Love so try swapping the word 'God' for 'Love' (maybe the grey beardy man still lurks!) so that it is Love that made man, Love provides for man and Love grants man unparalleled freedom and Love says 'I have created you to be like me, as my beloved children. I give you the whole world in which you your children and your children's children may rule and reign, and I also give you your freedom. Just trust me and believe in my uncompromising goodness as your father creator, that the whole of creation bears witness to, and follow my direction on the matter of this particular tree'...

...To which the actions of Adam and Eve were a resounding "No".

Now this is where the proverbial tyre hits the road and the honesty requirement comes in:

This could all be just some fable or fairy tale if we are not prepared to honestly look deep into our past and ask ourselves some uncomfortable questions? Looking back over our days on planet earth do the core principles of this story have any parallels in our own lives? Has the world firstly belittled God in our eyes, made us mistrustful of him, maybe we even questioned the very existence of such a being after hearing other voices and ideas exalting themselves against the concept of a personal, loving God that we unquestioningly attributed authority to?

Could we be prepared to even consider admitting to having been in situations where our conscience says no, but out of a desire to satisfy our physical frame, or a desire to have some attractive thing, or because of pride and the prospect of gaining what we perceived at the time as a promotion of status we have knowingly pushed aside our conscience and said "yes"?

Following the character assassination of God in the garden, the debut pairing failed to fully appreciate, and give reverence to, how their creator was providing for them both physically and spiritually since they came into being. Now, although nothing outwardly has changed, inwardly having chosen wrong over right and deciding to become a law unto themselves they haven't spiritually camped in some middle ground between God and "not God". To do that they would have had to call God in on the conversation and listened to God and the devil put forth their individual case on the matter of the tree before doing anything. But rather they made their decision quickly and chose "not God" over God and graduated from their first class in following a teaching contrary to that of their maker, provider and source.

Creation tells us that the eyes of Adam and Eve were opened after eating the fruit. To which the counter action is unable to reverse the act of them seeing. Can we, as uncomfortable as it is, be brave enough to wind the clock back and accept that we are intuitively aware when pushing our conscience aside like this and knowingly doing wrong, that we incur a cost to the detriment of our peace accompanied by the realisation that we are powerless by ourselves to undo what has been done?

Genesis 3: 8-9
New International Version (NIV)

Then the man and his wife heard the sound of the LORD God as he was walking in the garden in the cool of the day, and they hid from the LORD God among the trees of the garden. But the LORD God called to the man, "Where are you?"

Physically, however, they are still in God's garden, where we are told God walks in the afternoon with them; inwardly, though, they have turned from him. They become painfully aware that they are at a black tie dinner and all of a sudden realize they are only wearing the tie! If they don't do something quick they'll be spotted! "I know", says Adam, "pass me those fig leaves!"

So now they are at a black tie dinner with the tie and a fig leaf – much better! Obviously this is not going to hide them at all but it is more likely to draw attention to the fact that they have fallen for the lie of the enemy.

We cannot stand before God trying to pretend that we are something different than what we are. We cannot bring our job titles or our bank balance or whatever we suppose is our prowess expecting it to curry favour with him. The God of the Bible, the God who made us, is all knowing (Omniscient) and all seeing (Omnipresent); he knows us intimately to the extent we are told that the hairs on our head are numbered and that he sees our very hearts.

Luke 12: 7
New International Version (NIV)

Indeed, the very hairs of your head are all numbered. Don't be afraid; you are worth more than many sparrows

1 Samuel 16: 7
New International Version (NIV)

But the LORD said to Samuel, "Do not consider his appearance or his height, for I have rejected him. The LORD does not look at the things people look at. People look at the outward appearance, but the LORD looks at the heart."

Mark 2: 8
New International Version - UK (NIV)

Immediately Jesus knew in his spirit that this was what they were thinking in their hearts, and he said to them, Why are you thinking these things?

So if we are going to speak with him we have to give up any ideas about hiding things from him. As Moses was told to remove his shoes before the burning bush, because the place he was standing was 'holy ground' so we must be prepared for a God that knows us intimately and requires that we relate to him with that understanding. Adam and Eve having spent time with God will have known this, yet after having clearly felt the reproach in their hearts of their actions decide upon a cover up. The covering that they prepared for themselves however is notable in its inadequacy. Notable also is that it was not Adam and Eve that sought a counsel with God with a view to amending the situation but, as throughout the Bible, it was God that came to them where they were.

Knowing what has happened, (remember his omnipresence), our loving Father in His question, "Where are you?", is not seeking Adam out, but offering His unique creation an opportunity to come clean!

Unwilling to be laid bare before God, the pair are in hiding. On being found, Adam sadly begins to exhibit characteristics of the new authority in his life, in that he indirectly accuses God of deception:

Genesis 3: 10
New International Version (NIV)

He answered, "I heard you in the garden, and I was afraid because I was naked; so I hid."

Adam and Eve had always been unclothed before God, and had met frequently. If the lack of suitable attire was a problem God would have said. But untrustworthy Adam and Eve, following their rebellion, are mistrustful of God. 'We're naked' they tell God, as if to say: we were with you all that time and you never told us! God gets straight to the point:

Genesis 3: 11
New International Version (NIV)

And he said, "Who told you that you were naked? Have you eaten from the tree that I commanded you not to eat from?"

It's clear that God is fully aware that they didn't come to this conclusion alone. The only obvious acceptable response at this point is a signed confession! Come on Adam you're caught red handed, there's no getting out of this now ... come on just hold your hands up...

Genesis 3: 12
New International Version (NIV)

The man said, "The woman <u>you</u> put here with me—she gave me some fruit from the tree, and I ate it."

Adam is no longer in a place to trust in the goodness of God for forgiveness and restoration. Even though, if he had of stopped to think about it, clearly a remedy in the form of the Tree of Life was available. With no small dose of arrogance (remember he is his own God now), rather than accept responsibility and seek God's mercy, he accuses God further (see the underline), questioning God's character (sounds familiar) whilst finding fault with and rejecting his greatest blessing, his wife, and absolving himself of blame in the process.

We must be clear that it was not the case that forgiveness and restoration were not available to Adam, the God of the Old Testament is the same as the one in the New, who loved unto death. Yet not once does Adam, following his unfaithfulness, ask anything of God but he only accuses his maker of the very crimes he himself is guilty of. The very fact that Adam and Eve were hiding from an omnipresent God is in itself representative of rebellion, in that it is tantamount to saying "we want nothing to do with you".

Note that the command to Adam was not: "If you eat from the tree you will die" which would have been more straightforward and akin to other commands such as "let there be light" and so on. But the "surely" in "you shall surely die" speaks of the reluctant acceptance of a Father who knows that if, against His desire, Man should choose to do that which he has been specifically told not to then on that path is the rejection and separation from his source and the guidance of the one who loves him more than any other who has his best interests at heart. From here, God knows that the deterioration that follows would inevitably bring about his eventual spiritual death. The "surely" then denotes this not as a command but rather foretelling of the outcome which we are beginning to see here being played out.

So let us ask then most seriously, and with great solemnity, does this story have any echo in our own lives and in what we see of the general attitudes of mankind as expressed in our modern day culture? Certainly mankind is still capable of good deeds, which is not in contradiction with the Creation narrative's description of us as being created in the likeness of God, but what of the attitude of our heart toward God?

Do we live out our lives humbly in reverence to plain truth that there is so much that we don't and will never understand, or are we boastful and eager to depose God because of the little we do know?

Do we place unwarranted importance on possessing alluring objects and increased status, or are we keeping ourselves grounded in the truth of our finite existence?

Do we seek to build up the spiritual man within our deteriorating frame, or are we preoccupied with indulging the senses while we can?

Do we quickly accept responsibility for our mistakes, or do we offer excuses and seek to attribute blame for our own failings elsewhere? Certainly the appeal of Eastern philosophies, or teachings that fall under the umbrella of "New Age" beliefs, that I was once a proponent of, was the promise of freedom from anxiety that a God who required no personal accountability for wrongdoing offered. An offer that Eastern-based philosophies ironically share with atheistic teachings which if we were to take the Gospel as "Gospel" could go some ways to explaining their popularity.

Admittedly finding it excruciatingly difficult to say sorry and admit when we have been found to be in the wrong is a character trait I have become painfully aware of in myself and others of my gender. A particular favourite of mine is "I'm sorry" followed by the inevitable "...but". But what? "But I'm not sorry at all and it was actually your fault!" Anything after the first "but "and it just really isn't sorry at all in truth.

As a consequence of pride mixed with an unwholesome arrogance, rather than accept responsibility for being stupid enough to go against what our hearts already warned us of and despite the resulting sinking feeling within, aren't we more likely to find fault with God for the disturbance of our feng shui, over and above our change for the worse within becoming the catalyst to us seeking God and his hand for a remedy to our situation?

Again we must be clear that it's not just the action of doing what they had explicitly been told not to do, and warned against, but the following 'two fingers up' attitude when God seeks a counsel with the pair that is evident of the poison of their own rebellion and the new teaching they're under working its way through the spiritual bloodstream of the pair, paralysing their ability to move back to the place where they trusted God, that is symptomatic of the state of play within the heart of man in full rejection of his creator.

This then is the uncomfortable fundamental message of these passages of scripture. Although mankind is God's designated representative, like any would-be partnership we are not able to function when the executor of the command is essentially opposed to the author. As a result there has needs been a separation between them.

Would we continue to partner with someone in a venture who although having invested much in them in the past, we find them now opposed to our plans, acting against our purposes and having no desire to heed our direction?

Mistrustful of God's character, slanderous and untrustworthy, unyielding to his requests, holding in contempt His goodness and working now against His will, Adam and Eve could no longer stay in God's "garden of delight" lest they should gain eternal life whilst in their current state through eating from the Tree of Life and thus wreak eternal havoc upon God's creation.

God however would still be available to them outside and Adam was right on one thing, they did now require a covering to stand before God. God provides a more adequate temporary solution than the fig leaves by clothing the pair in animal skins. Yet the permanent solution for Adam and Eve's rebellion and the end of the deceptive power of God and mankind's common enemy is spoken of also before the episode is over.

Genesis 3: 15
New International Version (NIV)

*"... And I will put enmity between you and the woman, and
between your offspring and hers;
he will crush your head, and you will strike his heel."*

Where are we heading?

This is first taste of the Gospel (good news) of Jesus in the Bible,
when God tells Eve that one of her offspring (the original verb is
singular) will be the enemy of the serpent, and although the
serpent may bruise the heel of this individual, this individual will
crush his head! This speaks of the disempowerment of Satan,
mankind's accuser, and the silencing of his voice within the heart of
a restored mankind.

In accepting the serpent's teaching as guidance for their lives in
place of God's, Adam and Eve were placing all the immense power
and the promises that were gifted to them, of ruling and reigning,
under the authority of a being that hates God and seeks to destroy
all His works, them included (the second generation of biblical
humanity sees the first murder), whilst possessing a serious God
complex himself.

Failing to tempt Jesus in the wilderness with the same three
weaknesses of man that brought about the original fall, we read of
Satan gloating of his Garden deception.

Luke 4: 6
New International Version (NIV)

*And he said to him, "I will give you all their authority and
splendour; it has been given to me, and I can give it to anyone I
want to".*

The birth, life, death and resurrection of Jesus Christ is the final physical love letter of God to wayward mankind and the outward display of the triumph of God. His death and resurrection fulfilled many things which we will discuss in the chapter 'So someone died on a cross 2000 years ago and...?' One of these we will touch on now is that the covering provided for Adam and Eve has been now been made permanent through Jesus whose name is now the spiritual covering in which we are assured of access into His presence. (No need to kill a local sheep and ascend the nearest hill with its carcass on your back then!)

God, throughout the Bible, is calling us to walk not as Adam walked but to trust in his uncompromising goodness that he may restore us to our rightful position. In Jesus he reaps the death that all humanity together has sown, clearing the way for us to return to Him. This is the "good news" or gospel: that the chasm of the multiplication of rejections upon rejections of God since the beginning of humanity, that we collectively and as individuals, have placed between ourselves and God has, in Jesus, been bridged by God Himself and the enemy that outwits us at every turn has been disempowered.

As a result, the happenings in the Garden of Eden, I would propose, are more relevant now (that is, in New Testament times) to humankind than ever before. As personally, like Adam and Eve, we each individually have just one short journey, one choice, one step to take to be restored to our rightful position as children of our kingly creator.

In-line with the teachings of the Creation narrative, the fact that many of us, including myself, have taken issue with the Bible for being resolute in its message that we are wrong and God is right, and the onus for being reunited with God is with us, serves only to confirm the deep and lasting truth of these passages. Truly outside, of some calamitous situation or life changing event, unless we are especially sensitive, rarely are we willing to vacate the throne of our lives and seek the forgiveness of God through, as the Amplified Bible puts it, "heartily amending of our ways, with abhorrence of past wrongdoings". Consequently Jesus spent very little time attempting to convince the wise, the rich and successful or the comfortable of the authenticity of His ministry. The biblical word for the preparatory work within the heart of Man, and what was lacking from our foliage wearing forerunners, is repentance. But this is one of those words that, like others, has become stigmatised for many, conjuring images of some wild looking miserable man with a sandwich board in the centre of town heckling passing shoppers with wrath and condemnation.

Yet the God who is calling us is far from wrathful, He is in His words "gentle, meek and humble in heart", He is the one who showered forgiveness upon the very ones who drove the nails into His hands and feet.

Matthew 11: 29
New International Version (NIV)

Take my yoke upon you and learn from me, for I am gentle and humble in heart, and you will find rest for your souls.

Luke 23: 34
New International Version (NIV)

"Father, forgive them, for they do not know what they are doing."

Choosing to seek the mercy of God (placing our trust in his uncompromising goodness) with a repentant heart (acknowledging our fault) through God's prescribed method, Jesus, (in obedience to his plan rather than ours) and asking him for a second chance at living life as he would have us live it, under his guidance, is, as I am trying to highlight by the bracketed text, the reversal of our Adam-like decision to mistrust God, blame him, and become a law unto ourselves.

Nevertheless, as wide as God opens his arms He still created us free and we remain so: returning to Him has to be our choice. "Where are we heading?" individually is, as always, up to us.

In the words of the ex Private Eye Editor Malcolm Muggeridge: "Never forget only dead fish swim with the stream".

Or in the words of Jesus:

John 21: 18
New International Version (NIV)

"... Very truly I tell you, when you were younger you dressed yourself and went where you wanted; but when you are old you will stretch out your hands, and someone else will dress you and lead you where you do not want to go."

Although the lessons of Creation seem, at times, a bitter pill to swallow, at times I pray that all of us including myself would persevere in them.

The Devil, Hell and All That Scary Stuff

I mentioned in the first chapter that even after accepting Jesus at the New Testament Church of God in Leeds it was still another year of wrestling with various aspects of Christian teaching and visiting other churches to hear their take on the Bible before I committed to attending New T full-time. A major catalyst to this year in the wilderness was the events of one Sunday afternoon:

My wife must have been away that weekend with the boys as I had attended church alone that day and was able to accept the invitation of an older white gentlemen and his wife to go for lunch with them. It was a reluctant acceptance as, to be honest, I preferred the unhindered friendliness and laid back attitude of the Caribbean members of the church over the white folks, whom I had pigeonholed early on as Billy Graham wannabes. Yet confronted with the offer of lunch, and my new acquaintance having picked up on my hesitancy to accept his offer, English politeness kicked in and I decided to try laying aside my prejudices and to give the couple the benefit of the doubt.

We travelled by car for sit down Fish and Chips, right up my street, in some part of Leeds I was unfamiliar with. What wasn't "right up my street" was the couples' insistence on us joining hands and praying before we ate, which in such a public setting made me more than a little uncomfortable. Following that though everything went alright, he told me his history and I shared a bit about my circumstances, he offered encouragement and so on. Leaving the restaurant we had agreed that they would drop me off at the local train station from where I could get into town and then make my way home. Half way through the journey, without warning, my host, as casually as mentioning the weather forecast, drops into the conversation some warning to me about the DEVIL!!! Of all things!

Instantly my worst fears were confirmed: I was in a car with Billy Graham and his Mrs, any second they were going to tell me that if I stopped going to church I was going to burn in Hell! I don't even remember exactly in what context the subject was brought up and it doesn't really matter, the very fact that he had even attempted to introduce such a poisonous notion into the conversation made me very pissed off which I made known when we reached the station by offering the briefest of disdain-filled goodbyes ...

The "poison of the notion" was of course, as everyone knows, that it is the very idea that there is a force for evil at work in the world itself that is the greatest evil of all! Much of the beliefs that I had taken on board up to that point concurred and I was in no hurry to reject all that I had studied, even John Lennon knew it: *"Imagine there's no heaven. It's easy if you try. No hell below us. Above us only sky. Imagine all the people living for today"*. This duality in our thinking that is part of western philosophy, all this good and evil heaven and hell stuff, has done more harm than good is what he is saying! If we would only train ourselves, each individually, not to think about what the "big tomorrow" may hold and live each day and each moment at a time, casting these mental and spiritual burdens aside, then the resulting effect, like a pebble dropped into a pond, would reverberate through our societies and civilisation bringing peace in place of perpetual conflict and love in place of hate.

What I wanted at this stage in my walk with Jesus was to simply add a hearty "Amen" to the end of all this. I mean, Jesus was the great wise man, he even looked a bit like John Lennon, surely they were on the same page really weren't they? I was sure all that fire and brimstone stuff was in the Old Testament anyway and the New Testament stuff that was really important is all Jesus walking on the waves and speaking about peace and love isn't it?

It didn't take much time spent with a Bible before this standpoint became unsustainable as, much to my own frustration and disappointment, it quickly became apparent that Jesus was no Eastern mystic and that the teaching of an enemy at work within the world and the concept of alternative destinations at the end of this life are far more than a side issue, or sub plot, in his work.

Matthew 10: 28-31
New International Version (NIV)

Do not be afraid of those who kill the body. Rather, be afraid of the One who can destroy both soul and body in hell. Are not two sparrows sold for a penny? Yet not one of them will fall to the ground apart from the will of your Father. And the very hairs on your head are all numbered. So don't be afraid; you are worth many sparrows.

Throughout his recorded life he made persistent references to this personality to which he had enmity. His earthly ministry began by being tempted in the desert by the Devil for forty days and forty nights and he openly proclaimed the ruling religious leaders of the time to be 'Children of the Devil'! Prior to his death it was Satan that "entered in" to Judas Iscariot!

As unattractive as these notions were, as time went on simply ignoring it wasn't going to make it go away. None of the churches I visited around Leeds fused the teachings of the east and Jesus as I'd hoped and those that were something like it were lacking the presence of God that I had experienced at New T. If I was going to take this seriously then I couldn't just pick and choose the bits I liked. Reading the Gospels, one thing was immediately apparent: Jesus wasn't inclined towards speaking casually; everything he said and did was filled, even overflowing, with purpose and meaning.

John 12: 49
New International Version (NIV)

For I did not speak on my own, but the Father who sent me commanded me to say all that I have spoken.

So he meant it. But what did Jesus mean when he spoke of things like Satan and Hell?

Is it then just perhaps a well intentioned lie designed to prod us in to Heaven? In other words: Is Jesus just trying to chase us in to

Heaven through fear of the Devil?

Well that doesn't really add up, as the quote in the first chapter from John 6: 44 expresses. A foundational teaching of faith in Jesus is that nobody can come to the knowledge of God except when it is God himself that draws them. And God is Love:

1 John 4: 8
New International Version (NIV)

Whoever does not love does not know God, because God is love.

So what is it then?

Is it a trick?

Well we have gone through the whole Adam and Eve thing so we should understand that we are not to consider that God would be lying:

Numbers 23: 19
New International Version (NIV)

God is not human, that he should lie,
*   not a human being, that he should change his mind.*
Does he speak and then not act?
*   Does he promise and not fulfill?*

Certainly as merely a concept or idea of an ultimate reality behind the veil of this world, these aspects of Jesus' teaching are not going to win many admirers! In truth I am personally still unsure as to what kind of person it takes to willingly accept these teachings without any kind of revelation. Ordinarily if we're just shopping for beliefs then our inquiry may understandably be quickly curtailed at this juncture, particularly in today's spiritual marketplace where to our fallen Adam-like nature and attitudes there are better offers on the table with far less responsibilities. In addition we all like to believe that we are fundamentally good, and all this talk of evil and consequences can cause us to reject biblical teaching out of a sense of indignation at the suggestion that we are otherwise.

Actually for once we have a case here; as outlined in the last chapter, we were created to be a lot more than just good. In the biblical scheme of things we were created by a creator, who is holy, to be holy ourselves. And when we were made, we and all creation were declared as good, remember?

Yes we are created by God for good, which is evident by our mere existence and not only good but much more besides. Our problem as outlined in the last chapter is our spiritually inherited willingness to evict God from our lives. If we were able to accept the message of the Garden of Eden from the last chapter then the idea of journeying inwards to find God proposed by "new-age" beliefs would be a bit like searching high and low in your house for a pair of shoes you threw out yourself yesterday.

How new are these ideas though? By the Apostle Paul's day, the Greek philosopher Socrates had already summed up the redundancy of intelligent self-enquiry, in terms of its ability to enable us to reach beyond ourselves. Asked "Who is the wisest man in Greece" he famously replied "All I know is that I know nothing". In this statement he was expressing that he had come to realize that much of his thinking was based on past experience which wasn't able to prepare him for the unknown of the coming moment. He had reached the dead end of self-enquiry that Greek philosophers share with Eastern philosophers, that after the psychological value of understanding the driving forces behind our actions is all used up, we may be a bit more aware of what motivates our behaviour but we are in truth no nearer to coming into contact with God.

(If you're as unfamiliar with biblical terminology as I was then in the quote below a 'Gentile' means anyone who isn't Jewish.)

1 Corinthians 2: 18-25
New International Version (NIV)

For the message of the cross is foolishness to those who are perishing, but to us who are being saved it is the power of God. For it is written:

"I will destroy the wisdom of the wise;
the intelligence of the intelligent I will frustrate."

Where is the wise person? Where is the teacher of the law? Where is the philosopher of this age? Has not God made foolish the wisdom of the world? For since in the wisdom of God the world through its wisdom did not know him, God was pleased through the foolishness of what was preached to save those who believe. Jews demand signs and Greeks look for wisdom, but we preach Christ crucified: a stumbling block to Jews and foolishness to Gentiles, but to those whom God has called, both Jews and Greeks, Christ the power of God and the wisdom of God. For the foolishness of God is wiser than human wisdom, and the weakness of God is stronger than human strength.

If we are fundamentally good though where do all the problems come from? Surely left to our own devices everything would just be hunky dory wouldn't it? God is good we are good, creation is good?

Yet all is not well with us and the world.

Looking at that last statement logically, if we are unwilling to accept the existence of another force at work, one of these "goods" must really be bad mustn't it if we are to explain the state of the world?

Either: God is not really good; mankind is fundamentally degenerate; or it is the created world that is somehow spiritually toxic.

The most popular, obviously, is to blame or deny the existence of a creator, leaving the way open for a multitude of theories. Jesus however certainly didn't mince his words concerning the source of the existence of evil in the world:

John 14: 30-31
Amplified Bible (AMP)

I will not talk with you much more, for the prince (evil genius, ruler) of the world is coming. And he has no claim on Me. [He has nothing in common with Me; there is nothing in Me that belongs to him, and he has no power over Me.]

But [Satan is coming and] I do as the Father has commanded Me, so that the world may know (be convinced) that I love the Father and that I do only what the Father has instructed Me to do. [I act in full agreement with His orders.] Rise, let us go away from here.

John 8: 44
New International Version (NIV)

You belong to your father, the devil, and you want to carry out your father's desires. He was a murderer from the beginning, not holding to the truth, for there is no truth in him. When he lies, he speaks his native language, for he is a liar and the father of lies.

So what are we left with?

Well eventually we may have to try just taking Jesus at his word, meaning that we will try entertaining the notion that Jesus was speaking soberly and without metaphor about something which it is important for us to understand. For the remainder of this chapter we shall be exploring what that might mean.

What?

Should we be looking out for some marauding red painted man who's seeking out any opportunity to stick us with his trident then?

Well no. Understanding the Bible as being primarily a spiritual guide, the enemy of God who is (as in the garden episode) seeking to usurp God's place of authority in the heart of mankind (to be as God), in imitation of God, exists also as a spiritual entity.

Now in an age where we entrust the welfare of our minds to psychologists, talking about a spiritual entity trying to influence you sounds a bit vague and not something that should really concern us too much. To put it another way, what we are really talking about, as in the Garden of Eden with Eve, is a word, or to be more descriptive an argument, proposal, or idea put to you for action by yourself, that if fulfilled would place you in direct opposition to God's will for your life.

Before we get on to how this suggestion may find itself as part of our thinking, let us be assured that, yes, God has a purpose for each one of us that he created us specifically for.

Jeremiah 29: 11
New International Version (NIV)

For I know the plans I have for you," declares the Lord, "plans to prosper you and not to harm you, plans to give you hope and a future.

In addition, each of us created by God, intuitively possess within us God's moral code which, once we've reached a responsible age, acts as a kind of early warning system within our hearts.

Romans 2: 14-15
New International Version - UK (NIVUK)

(Indeed, when Gentiles, who do not have the law, do by nature things required by the law, they are a law for themselves, even though they do not have the law. They show that the requirements of the law are written on their hearts, their consciences also bearing witness, and their thoughts sometimes

accusing them and at other times even defending them.)

If we can really forget about the trident carrying moustachioed red chap stabbing us, then where might we need to turn our attention to, to be on guard against ideas or arguments that are contrary to the will and teaching of God? Bearing in mind that God has created mankind to be holy.

Leviticus 11: 44
New International Version - UK (NIVUK)

I am the Lord your God; consecrate yourselves and be holy, because I am holy. Do not make yourselves unclean by any creature that moves along the ground.

1 Thessalonians 3: 13
New International Version (NIV)

May he strengthen your hearts so that you will be blameless and holy in the presence of our God and Father when our Lord Jesus comes with all his holy ones.

The question then, put another way, is: where might we find propositions that are contrary to living a life of holiness?

Well when we put it like that...!

All around us, every day, to be honest. Particularly in the media rich societies of the west, where our consumer society is persistently seeking to highjack our hopes and dreams by presenting ideals at a frantic rate that offer heavenly blessings from worldly pleasures. Where our natural attraction to the opposite sex is employed to add allure to just about anything and the miracle of photography and the moving image opens a back door into our consciousness; a walk through the modern city a battleground for our attention and our allegiance.

(The back door I'm alluding to is that noted by pioneering French photographer Henri Cartier-Bresson, that when the brain sees a photograph it firstly perceives it as reality and only secondly as an image. For example, an image of a scantly glad women painted on the side of a house in the war years would excite the local cricket team but a heavy dose of imagination would be required, not so with a photograph.)

Although I'm not sure how 'indirect' these influences really are, for the time being we will refer to the aforementioned influences as such.

Equally there are direct influences or, to put it in everyday language, we talk to ourselves. I'd like to point out here though, before anyone throws the baby out with the bathwater, that I'm not saying the trident carrying red chap is present at every mini-conference we have with ourselves, I am only proposing that he has the capacity to attend. Alright stay with this now, I know this is starting to get a little heavy.

Hopefully, facing up to the reality that there are conflicting arguments within our conscience is not too disturbing. What I am trying to explain with regards to what the Bible teaches us about these conflicting voices is that we are not the source of all these. (Phew! We can cancel the appointment to see the psychiatrist.) Obviously we generate our own ideas as, like our Father, we are creative beings with freedom not simply a void waiting to be filled. Jesus is telling us through this teaching though that there are, in addition to our own thoughts, direct and indirect influences on our thinking, coming from spiritual sources that work against the purposes of God and we should not be ignorant of these.

Hopefully a bit of fiction might give us a break and help make things a little clearer and easier to swallow:

The worst best friend you ever had!

David was fifteen and lived with his parents and younger twin sisters. It was the summer holidays and his friend Loz who had just moved to the area was due over. It was a reconciliatory meeting really, rather than a standard visit, as David's Dad had nearly half-killed Loz only a couple of weeks ago when, after a sequence of bizarre petty thefts from the building site that was to be their new house where items such as toilet seats and taps had been stolen, David's Dad had snuck up on what he presumed to be the culprit only to find that the subsequently unconscious intruder was in fact the mannish 15 year old, Loz, looking for keys he'd lost earlier in the day. Although David's Dad still had his doubts, influenced partly by the guilt of having knocked out what, by law, is technically a child, he gave Loz, and his alibi, the benefit of the doubt although he would tell David from then on not to bring him in the house. Nevertheless, Loz continued to be a regular at the door and David, even though it wasn't the most natural of friendships, had little else to do.

Polar opposites would, in truth, be a better description: Loz, full of urban culture with years of fending for himself and living by his own rules behind him, contrasted starkly with David's life where the only contact with anything urban was through the television which was still regulated by his parents!

Yet the zeal with which his new found, self-proclaimed "best boy" spoke about life in the city was infectious and soon David's imagination, and not to mention his hormones, were captured with visions of police chases, booze and drug fuelled parties and "fit birds". "You're missing out living here Dave", Loz would tell him, "As soon as I'm 16 I'm going back as long as I've not gone mad through sheer bloody boredom here by then".

Perhaps David was missing out? He began to muse. The country life had always been his Dad's dream, not his. Dad had been building the "dream" house for the family for the past six years and it was nearly ready to move into. Separate rooms for the girls and two bathrooms to put an end to the nightly ritual of arguing, and lots more space generally. Loz nicknaming the house "Alcatraz" and his daily warning to "Dave" to get out "before the old Tyrant locks you up for good in there" had certainly cooled David's enthusiasm for the project. "That's a bloody life sentence he's building for you there that is" was another of Loz's favourite assessments of David's future. However, David had started to become a little weary of late of simply laughing off these remarks which had become more persistent than he had expected they would.

That day was like most others – the pair had little to do. David was avoiding his Dad who would more than likely have him wheel barrowing something or other if he caught sight of him. "I know just the bird I could fix you up with Dave you know if we were in the city". "Really?" replied David, sarcastically, who had also started to question whether anything Loz said was in fact true. There was a pause while Loz fiddled with his phone as he did at regular intervals followed by him speaking in a hushed tone to somebody like he was about to pull off the biggest international drug deal of all time. This was generally just part of spending any amount of time with him. "Do you wanna speak to her then?" Loz thrust his mobile phone towards him and David could hear a girl's voice coming from the handset.

"Hello?",

"Hellooo?",

"Loz are you pissing around?" came the girl's voice from the phone.

David took the phone from Loz and spoke?

"Hi, err hello", David stumbled, "How are you?"

It was cringy but to David's relief the girl on the other end of the line found his awkwardness endearing.

As it turned out, this was not a spur of the moment thing, Loz had told this girl all about David and sent her pictures of him and everything. What's more, she had only agreed to speak to him because she had decided he was "fit" and wondered if there might be a chance of meeting up sometime.

Loz wasn't stupid and knew that David's interest in his world had been wearing thin. While it was just mere talk David would always take everything he said with a heavy pinch of salt, Loz figured David's Dad would have told him as much.

Seemingly vindicated by the latest turn of events, Loz assumed charge of their plans for the rest of the day. David, overwhelmed with gratitude, dropped his usual suspicions and followed along whilst plying Loz with questions about the girl on the phone. She was called Mel and from what he could tell she was everything he said she was. Scrolling through the photos on his phone it was clear that Loz really wasn't the fantasist David had had him down for. Some of the stuff on his phone could have got him arrested for sure. Handing back the phone after some time had passed, David noticed that his friend had all the while been busying himself by inscribing a huge love heart with the words "Dave + Mel" into one of David's Dad's paving slabs for the new house.

"What have you done!"

"My Dad will go mental!", screamed David.

"Alright calm down, don't be a dick" retorted Loz, who was used to being congratulated for vandalism by his followers, not reprimanded.

"You don't understand!" said David.

"I understand alright", began Loz, "you don't want to get into trouble with Daddy!" "Get a grip Dave, you need to sort you're old man out and stop him treating you like a kid".

If Loz had come out with that this morning, David would have probably cut Loz loose for good, but since it had become clear that day that Loz had more to offer than just tall tales, plus of course Mel...

"What would you know?" he replied. Loz, to his knowledge, had never had a Dad, he'd never spoken about him anyway.

"I know about how to get dick heads off your case, that's what I know" replied Loz angrily. Whether this was a reference to his own Dad, David's Dad or David himself was unclear, but the ferocity with which it was delivered meant that it was most definitely the end of the exchange and Loz had come out the victor.

After an uncomfortable silence David began strolling over to the paving slab propped up against the wall then like lightning proceeded to launch a classic Mortal Combat style flying kick at the slab which split in two and fragmented further as it hit the floor. Loz, grabbing a second slab, copied the move adding a twist and karate movie style sound effects he missed his footing and landed flat on his back into a pile of wet sand. The laughing and general arsing around that followed was liberating for David. Branded officially "mental" by Loz, the highest accolade Loz was ever known to use, the pair hid the pieces of "broken Alcatraz" underneath masses of building sand. The boys went their separate ways closer than ever with plans for the big meeting with Mel plus friend in place for the weekend.

The following morning David was rudely awoken by the sound of shouting from his parents. Stood on the landing at the top of the

stairs he had already taken a deep breath to tell them to shut up when he suddenly realised he was the subject of their confrontation.

"Don't wake him up. I'm sure he has a reasonable explanation", his Mum was saying.

"If I find it's anything to do with that Loz character I kill him!", his

Dad warned.

It would appear that the previous night's antics had entered the public arena, "just the morning for a lay in", thought David to himself.

After snoozing a while he got himself dressed stealthily as not to give any indication to his parents below that he was awake and waited. He knew that his Dad would at some point want to catch the news headlines on the front room telly, and then if all went to plan he might be able to make his escape. Hedging his bets that it would be the headlines at 10 o'clock, David began to make his way down the stairs, avoiding the third from the bottom step that always creaked like it was stolen from a pirate ship. When David was younger and his Dad was in a considerably better mood than he was right now he would shout "Shiver me timbers" whenever he stood on it in a mock pirate voice and rush into David's room diving on him to tickle him until he surrendered. David's thoughts had turned to pondering on what exactly had changed since then when, right on cue, on went the telly. David opened the door to the kitchen, grabbing an apple on the way through, he made for the back door with an innocently melodic "Hi Mum, Hi Dad". His mum's own subsequent "David?" was drowned out by his own "Bye Mum, Bye Dad" and the sound of the back door slamming shut.

Once outside, David grabbed his bike, he knew he would have to face them sooner or later, but he preferred later to sooner.

For the first time in their entire but brief friendship David decided tocall on Loz, maybe he could provide moral support or tips on how to get out of it, at least a laugh might take his mind off of the inevitable confrontation that had begun to loom all the more now he was out of the house.

Pulling up at a very ordinary house in the village, his knock at the door was answered by younger woman than he expected, smoking with a toddler trying to make a break for it the moment the door had opened. "Come here you evil little bugger!" she said grabbing the baby who began laughing which then quickly turned to screaming when he realised that his destination was behind the bars of the stair gate attached to the entrance of the kitchen down the hall.

I was just wondering if Loz was in, enquired David politely.

"Who's asking?", came the unusually suspicious reply.

David could hear the TV and the voices of another man and another woman laughing in the front room.

"My names David, I'm a friend of his, I live just outside the village."

"David is it?" she mocked in familiar way that made David a little uncomfortable.

"You mean you're Dave are you? Finally gracing us with your presence.... ahh... he's not here."

A perturbed David turned to leave.

"He's giving evidence today or hasn't he told you?", she fired out as David was half way up the drive. "As long as he doesn't mess up, this time next week we'll all be back home."

The rather dumbfounded David hopped on his bike and sped off to waste the best of the day catching the sun in a hedge bottom between the village and home. Away from Loz's house, the shock of the encounter with his mum soon became a blip of unfamiliarity in the context of a very familiar day.

Due to Loz's self-declared independence from the authority of his parents, David wasn't too concerned about the report or for that matter the behaviour of his mum. In fact, rather than cast doubt upon their friendship it had served only to confirm Loz's version of events: that his friend was to all intense purposes independent, and despite her boasting David was no doubt privy to more of Loz's life than she was.

Inevitably, hunger drove David home by around three. Attempting to repeat the success of his exit but in reverse he entered through the kitchen at the back making a break for the stairs and his room, but his mum, in a much sterner voice than before, halted him in his steps. He had clearly lost her as an ally in what was about to take place.

"Why don't you tell me why we're here David?" his Dad began.

David remained silent, avoiding eye contact with his Dad.

The silence was interrupted by his sisters giggling and chasing each other down the stairs. Before they reached the kitchen, his Mum met them at the foot of the stairs telling them to calm down and go back upstairs for a while to play quietly. When the third step creaked the second of the twins joyfully cried out "shiver me timbers" and proceeded to chase her sister into their bedroom where the giggling continued.

David, forgetting himself, couldn't help but smile.

"I'm glad you've got something to smile about son, 'cause I don't feel much like smiling at the moment with a half finished patio and a mate with a broken foot because you and that so called FRIEND of yours think it's a good idea to smash my building materials up" said

David's Dad.

When they had begun work at the house that morning the digger they had hired to move the sand had scooped up part of one of the slabs and dropped it on David's uncle's foot.

"It's wasn't anything to do with Loz! I knocked them over by accident messing about!" was the extent of David's defence.

"I suppose you then pushed the broken pieces together and wrote on them after did you?" David hadn't thought his story through.

"All I know is you never did anything like this before he turned up, so you're not to see him anymore" continued his Dad.

"You can't do that, I'm nearly sixteen years old! I can choose my own friends thanks!" David complained

"Oh well seeing as you're a big man now, you won't mind do a bit of hard graft and take the place of your uncle whose foot your antics are responsible for breaking. On site you can choose who your friend will be: Mr Shovel or Mr Wheelbarrow or both maybe? And the money you would've earned can pay for the slabs you smashed. Work starts Monday and if I see you anywhere near the site before then you'll lose all your privileges".

This was about the best that David could've expected, he was almost relieved because he'd worked on site before and, although it was hard work, today was Friday and they never worked weekends which left him free to keep his appointment with Mel.

"You're also grounded this weekend" concluded his Dad as he left David sat at the kitchen table with his Mum as a silent observer to the whole thing.

The mild mannered David then uncharacteristically began to well up with a mixture of anger, disappointment and self pity. Taking his emotions as a sign of regret his Mum attempted to console him by reminding him that his Dad "wasn't one to hold grudges" and "everything would be alright" as long as David just said sorry.

But David's response took his Mum by surprise. Wiping the tears from his eyes he looked his Mum straight in the face and said coldly "but I'm not sorry. I wish I'd have smashed more, then we might never have to move into that bloody monstrosity ever!" Irritated by his Mum's lack of awareness of the situation, David returned to his room reaffirming his hatred of their shared life's work and dream with the parting comment: "What do I wanna live in that bloody thing for the rest of my days for anyway."

Later that evening, another first... Loz sent David a text.

"Soz I wasn't about. Had stuff to sort. U out L8tr"

David replied explaining what had happened with the slabs. Loz promised to explain all the stuff his mum had spilled to David at their house tomorrow night when Mel and her friend came over from the city. Loz would come over and sneak up to David's house tomorrow and the walk in to the village would give him chance to explain.

Saturday, David avoided his family, feigning illness he took himself to bed for 7 from where he climbed out of the window to Loz who was holding a ladder from the building site and the pair made good their escape. This evening was the biggest thing that had ever happened to David, after tonight he might be working night-shifts on the house but he would deal with that later.

On the mile or so walk to the village, Loz had some fresh revelations for David. All had gone well and Loz and his Mum would be moving back to the city. Loz, it turns out, was in the village as part of a Police witness protection programme as he had been a witness to a murder that occurred some time ago.

Because of his Dad's insistence on keeping up to date with the news and his, how shall I put it... outspoken indignation at this particular case, David vaguely recollected the story: some old war veteran guys had disturbed a pair of burglars who paid him back for his bravery by sticking a kitchen knife in his chest. For Loz's part, he had accompanied an older friend of his to a derelict building to have a look round as a laugh. He knew nothing about a knife or that the house was even occupied.

As they were talking, the girls stepped out of a taxi. David recognised Mel from her photo, Loz casually continued the conversation: " I mean I knew he was a bit mental but not that, you know what I mean Dave" Loz concluded. "Yeah" answered David, who in truth had some more questions about the events but was trying his best to fit in now that the girls had arrived.

Amongst three people from the city, David became keenly aware that his dress and manner were markedly different to his peers. The girls were dressed so they looked at least 20 and Loz was old for his age anyway. Because of the manner of his exit, David hadn't been able to get changed and looked a bit like a pre-pubescent child pop sensation. Embarrassingly for David, this meant that the darkest corner of the local pub's beer garden would be the extent of their venture into the adult world. To add further embarrassment, he couldn't find the forty quid that he had brought out with him so Loz was buying all the drinks with what he called his first down payment from his Mum of his Police compensation money. It turned out that the other "mental" guy who stabbed the war veteran had tried to pin the whole thing on Loz and when the police had brought him in for questioning they managed to crack his head open! Officially cleared as of today, Loz already had his solicitor on the case.

A couple of pints of lager made David less self-conscious and Loz helped by bigging him up to the girls with a glorified version of the events of the previous night. Me,l with a couple of drinks down her, started to flirt with David, teasing him about his appearance firstly but then sensitively reassuring him that she thought it was "sweet" as she had done on the phone.

"You haven't told us yet what happened with your old man when you squared up to him yesterday Dave? His old man is a proper nutter, I reckon he only lives out here cause he's on the run or something" informed Loz. David laughed spitting out beer at the idea of his Dad as some gangland renegade. Loz wasn't joking: "He nearly killed me didn't he?" Reminded of Loz's ability to become ferociously serious David back tracked and agreed.

David recounted to the group the events of the preceding day exaggerating the dangers for effect: "I heard my Dad saying downstairs in the morning that if Loz was involved he was gonna kill me or him or both of us, so like Loz says he has got a temper, so I had to leg it to his house..." The picture that David painted of his life, with his re-telling, was of a die-hard free spirit imprisoned in a stiff and boring lifestyle by a mad dictator who, if it wasn't for the salvation of Loz, would have buried him under the patio long ago. The fantastical depiction of their lives in the sleepy English village had the desired effect on Mel who, making room for David following his return to the toilets, promptly sat on his knee teasing him for a few minutes before turning to snog him.

This behaviour had drawn the attention of the regulars of the Rose & Crown who alerted the management to the presence of the under-age drinkers among them. While the others promptly made for the exit Loz insisted on finishing his drink before delivering a barrage of unsubtly masked insults at the regulars underneath faked coughs as he left. To David and the girls it was priceless; to the regulars it was a blip of unfamiliarity in a very familiar evening.

Out of the pub, Loz , for whom it seemed the night was yet young, opened the doors of a small-hatchback down the street and the three worse for wear teenagers climbed in without hesitation. Loz drove erratically along the country lanes resting finally at the site of David's family's near completed house.

There the gang listened to music smoked and laughed. As the close of the evening became a reality, following a lengthy period of coping off in the car, everyone's attention turned to David and his situation. Loz was leaving before the end of next week. The girls had had a good time but were in no rush to return. In the city they were regulars in the nightclubs and even knew the bouncers on the door. Dave was of course invited, but after this there was no chance of him leaving the house let alone the village any time soon. Loz said that if it got too bad at home for David he had friends who would put him up until his compensation came through, then he was getting his own place.

The couples spent some time separately before Loz would have to take the girls back. Mel didn't have much to say. What was there to say? Their snogging was brought to an end by Loz's full beam and a beep from the horn. Mel jumped back in the car and with spinning tyres they were gone.

Stumbling through the building site back home it seemed to David as if he had been twenty for an evening and lived but now he would return to being treated like he was six and, more than likely, a life sentence as a punishment.

Half way home David squared up to Alcatraz, the constant aspersions cast upon his future by Loz swam round his head, "You shall not hold me", he declared to himself as, emboldened by his drunkenness, he picked up the nearest projectile launching with no particular purpose at the house in what to any outside observer would have appeared as laughable defiance.

If the sound of the kitchen window didn't sober him up then the appearance of flames inside the house did. David turned to home to see his Dad coming out of the house "David, is that you?!" shouted his Dad, who must have been woken by the car horn of Loz to have been outside by now. David turned heel and ran, his Dad followed until he too noticed the flames which had begun to take hold.

David in his panic rang Loz who met him surprisingly quickly just out of sight of the house.

"I've set the house on fire Loz!" spilled David in a panic.

"Why've you done that you dickhead!" came the unfeeling response from Loz.

David, caught unawares by the accusation, childishly moaned "I didn't mean to!" He was half expecting that Loz might congratulate him.

"You do realise that your Dad will actually kill both of us now don't you" said Loz.

"He's not going to kill you Loz, he's alright really but I can't go back there now!" David reprimanded.

"There you go again you little prick, what would you know, living out here eh! I've seen blokes like your Dad before and he is a proper, proper nutter. More to the point, if I'd of been building something for six years and some little dick weed came and burnt it down, I'd want to kill em, wouldn't you! And what about your sisters and your Mum it's meant to be their house too init..."

David to his shame hadn't thought of them.

"What were you thinking Dave?.... You're not right you."

Ashamed and now humiliated David certainly felt about six now!

"Well could I just stop with that mate of yours for a couple of nights at least" begged David. All he knew was he wanted to be away.

"What, are you gonna burn his house down too! As if he's gonna want you at his!"

"Please Loz, I'm begging you, just ask"

There was a pause before Loz agreed and drove them that night to the city. In the car the mood was dark unlike before. The music Loz selected and was purposefully nodding his head too was equally as grim, but David didn't dare ask him to change it. The girls had begun to pay the price for their earlier excesses and were dead to the world. Although David had cast glances toward Mel she hadn't once returned them.

Arriving at their apparent destination, round the back of some flats on the outskirts of the city, an older looking lad met Loz with a handshake as he stepped out of the car. The pair spoke for a couple of minutes, too quietly for David to hear, but he knew they were discussing him because at one point the lad, who could have passed for Loz's older brother, stared at Loz with a long cold unpleasant stare as if he was sussing him out. Loz motioned to David to get out of the car, first the older lad then joined by Loz started singing "He's the firestarter the twisted firestarter". David was wary enough now to realise that the joke was at his expense and not an invitation to exchange banter with his new acquaintance. Also it was immediately apparent that Loz and his friend were closer than David and Loz ever were:

"Right Dave I'm gonna head off, Stu here will sort you out, but if you even think of burning his place down he will kill you, now give us your phone a sec."

David passed Loz his mobile without question as he always had done.

"I'm having this now", said Loz coldly.

"What do you mean?" said David "Give me my phone".

"What I mean dickhead is you owe me for all the drinks I paid for tonight, the petrol and rent for Stu and I know you haven't got any money so I'm having your phone as part payment. You can square the rest up later", reasoned Loz.

"If you want to ring your Dad there's a phone box full of piss round the front of here, I'm sure he would love to speak to you. See you later..."

Loz jumped in the car and sped off, leaving David to the mercy of Stu and his flat. Stu said little as he led David to his flat and a weary looking empty room with a dirty mattress on the floor and security grills on the only window. At least it was summer so it wasn't cold.

David, tired and numbed by the intense drama of the evening, shut down and gave himself to sleep; maybe when he woke he would find himself at home in his own bed and realise it was all just a bad dream.

Morning arrived, however not with the twittering of birds like at home, but with the unwelcome sound of the arrival of Loz at the flat. He and Stu did their usual banter for a bit which gave David time to come round.

Following the fire last night, David's Dad had headed straight round to Loz's, with the police following a couple of minutes behind, where Loz had only minutes ago returned from dropping David off. "Where's my son you! Where is he!" demanded David's Dad, barging in the house and grabbing hold of Loz.

For once, Loz was glad of police intervention as they pulled David's Dad away from him and told him to leave it to them. Loz's mum new the drill though, Loz had been in most of the evening. "Most" was ambiguous enough to leave necessary gaps. Loz hadn't seen "Dave" for a while, not since he got grounded by "his old man". "Why what's going on?" questioned Loz.

It was officially a missing person's enquiry was all the officer would disclose. David's Dad who was hovering interrupted now, begging Loz to tell them where David was and if he did see him to tell David that he didn't care about the house, it could be rebuilt; and it wasn't that badly damaged anyway; but that he just wanted him home. "Tell him I won't even ground him Loz won't you" he pleaded," If he gets in contact tell him I've sorted it all out and he can come home, that his mum and sisters are worried about him and that we all love him ".

"Ok I'll do that for sure Mr Marshall" responded Loz wallowing in the power he now possessed over the "nobhead" who had once gotten the better of him by sneaking up on him from behind with a shovel that fateful evening. If he'd only had a moments forewarning

of his presence he could have done him with his knife like he did the other interfering old sod before.

Once David's Dad was out of earshot, Loz took hold of the opportunity to share his own ideas on the situation, whispering to the police that he wasn't sure whether David had run away from his Dad or was currently dwelling six feet under the patio, as "Dave was always running scared of his old man".

Sticking the knife in, Loz also told them that "Dave" had disclosed to him that he was abused by his Dad as a child and now he was getting older and angrier about it, had had a few run ins with his old man recently. "That will be why he wants to get to him before you lot". As he finished the sentence, David's Dad's car sped off into the night to the next of David's regular contacts. Loz was a master craftsmen that's for certain, the police knew, as he did, that there was a proven link between sexual abuse and kids starting fires.

For David, at least morning had brought the conviction that his only option was to return home. David didn't belong here with these people, that was for certain. Loz came in surprisingly upbeat and friendly for someone who ought not to expect anything of the sort from David in return. "Did you sleep alright in here Dave?" he asked in a tone that could have almost been mistaken for concern. "Stu, Stu! What's going on with this room, it's disgusting, what are you doing having my best boy in room like this, like a bloody animal!" To David's bemusement, the pair began to have a blazing row over the state of the room with Loz defending David's right for descent accommodation seeing as he was paying for it! Stu seemed equally as taken aback and bemused as David had been the previous night with this turn of events which saw him switch from celebrity to villain in the blink of an eye. Unbelievably, at the end of it all Stu was off to the newsagents downstairs to get David something to have for breakfast!

"Sorry about all this Dave, and sorry I was off with you last night I'm always like that when I'm coming down. All grumpy an' that; people *are always saying it. I had no idea this room was such a state, Stu told me it was sound and like an idiot I believed him." Handing David a twenty pound note, Loz told him that it was what was left of the money from pawning his phone which he could use it to get some toothpaste and stuff. A sober and more resilient David thanked Loz for the apology and informed Loz that he would be using the money to take himself home.*

After taking a long drag on a joint he'd just lit, Loz, from behind a cloud of smoke in a wheezy voice said: "You gonna try and sort things out with you old man then?"

"I don't know what I'm going to do really. I just want to go back now" answered David honestly.

"Like I always said Dave, you are a nutter" said the new, friendly relaxed Loz as he passed David the joint. David had never smoked a joint but he took it from Loz as though it was the most normal thing in the world. David took a couple of long drags on the joint as the solemn pair drew out what would be more than likely their final few minutes in one another's company.

A few exchanges of the joint later and after an inordinately long pause Loz resumed. "You are a nutter though Dave".

Another long pause, Loz passes the joint back to David who was starting to feel detached from reality as the cannabis began to affect him.

"I know you're a nutter because I've seen your old man last night and I would not want to face him the way he is right now."

David didn't move a muscle, yet his mind was ambushed suddenly with the horror of the previous night.

"I'm not telling you not to go back Dave you know but all I'm saying is that he was properly kicking off at our house last night

demanding that I tell him where you are 'cause he wanted to kill you. It's your sisters you see mate, they got injured in the fire when it spread to your house. They'll be alright but your Dad said... well I don't know if I should tell you this but, I swore to him that I didn't know where you were even though the police had to pull him off me, but he insisted that if I did see you that I was to tell you that it would be better for everyone if you stayed away 'cause he says that you're not his son anymore."

After another pause:

"I'll take you back in the car if you still want to go today Dave, but if it was me I would leave it a bit. It was only last night you burnt your own family's house down after all Dave?"

"Mel said she would come over later to see you"

"Do you still want to go back now?"

David sat on the floor with his head between his knees shook his head. He had made his bed and he was going to have to lay in it!

The End

Hopefully, at this stage, you get the point of what this story is really designed to illustrate.

Do we recognise the personality traits of this vile character Loz?

Are we uncomfortably familiar with this narrative? What is the source of this accusing voice within that has generations of teenagers hating themselves and generations of adults even still on the back foot? Is it a result, as some would suggest, of the overbearing presence of the unliveable standards of the Bible in society that somehow fuels such a reaction? Like all good lies, there is an element of truth in this in that we are always going to feel the reproach of any failure all the more severely when we have trespassed where we were specifically warned not to go. The fruit of Godly shame though is a repentant heart that brings us back to God who is able and willing to restore us, but the condemnations and accusation, peppered with aspersions cast against the goodness and trustworthiness of God, come from the enemy of our soul and not our Father.

John 3: 17
New International Version (NIV)

For God did not send his Son into the world to condemn the world, but to save the world through him.

The book of Revelation makes it clear:

Revelation 12: 10
New International Version (NIV)

Then I heard a loud voice in heaven say:

"Now have come the salvation and the power
  and the kingdom of our God,
  and the authority of his Messiah.
For the accuser of our brothers and sisters,
  who accuses them before our God day and night,
  has been hurled down."

As in the narrative above, having chosen to attribute authority to arguments that are contrary to the will of our Father, once the decisive step has been taken, of our own free will, our new companion is lightning fast to turn the tables and convict us of our unworthiness before a holy God and also loathed to relinquish his position as our chief advisor. Accusations, compliments, success, failure, thrills and spills, boredom, ease or turmoil whichever boot fits will be the one he will use at the opportune time to keep us down and separated from our Father. With ages of practice and full of vileness, deceit and guile, he is more than capable of manipulating the will of mankind away from his creator and the source of all his blessings.

John 8: 34-36
New International Version (NIV)

Jesus replied, "Very truly I tell you, everyone who sins is a slave to sin. Now a slave has no permanent place in the family, but a son belongs to it forever. So if the Son sets you free, you will be free indeed."

If the story were to continue then David would not be able to escape the clutches of Loz by himself. The deceptions and lies of Loz would move into overdrive as the course of David's life, manipulated by Loz's words, turned to crime and drugs. Loz's ultimate lie when the time was ripe would be to tell David that he had discovered that he was in fact adopted by his parents, reflecting the ultimate aim of our adversary to get us to completely disown even the faintest of notions about seeking our source.

If the Gospel were to make an appearance in the story then this would perhaps take the form of a message to David in a newspaper ad or something like that, which would tell him that his Father was not angry with him; that he had never stopped looking for him; his family missed him and that the house was rebuilt and his room was ready and waiting for him; phone number attached.

Loz would, of course, try and prevent David from seeing the advert. The question would be whether or not David had become too corrupted by his life under Loz to even want to return or believe the message at all. After a few years of life under Loz, David could be so detached from his former life and so utterly convinced of the truth of Loz's world that he may now believe it would have been better for his so-called Dad to have been inside the house when it caught fire! He may have even had chance meetings with his father in the city and felt the tug of home upon his heart, but then chosen the familiarity of the unwholesome comforts he now knows over a reunion with a life to which he is now a stranger.

Separated from God, time inevitably finds us multiplying our wrongdoing, therefore multiplying the ammunition our enemy has to throw at us and the allure of swapping a Holy, all-seeing, all-knowing God for something, anything, less intrusive becomes all the more alluring.

Yet stepping behind the veil of life at death, we will eventually be confronted with the truth of life where the secrets of men's hearts are exposed and the intent of our hearts will be weighed on the scales of God's justice. If we are in a state of enmity toward God then how are we going to be able to accept his rule or dwell in his presence? If we did not seek Him out to be reconciled with Him in life then shall we have a sudden change of heart in death?

If we believe that somehow on exiting this life we will be miraculously changed into who we were always meant to be then we might find it disappointing to discover that the Bible talks of no such promise.

Using the metaphor of the story again, consider how a David in his late forties, having spent a life addicted to hard drugs, a persistent petty criminal with convictions for grievous bodily harm and maybe even worse, could be expected instantly to slip into a world he has forgotten, a world that he has despised, mocked and resented increasingly as the years progressed? Not only would he not want to be there himself, David's father, if he had any sense wouldn't, for the sake of the family, have him there either.

Yet the metaphor I am using is not perfect by any stretch of the imagination and it isn't able to reflect the purity and holiness of the Kingdom of God or the extent of Man's rebellion against his creator.

To choose then to live eternally separate from the source of all our pleasures with the full knowledge of God as the source of these, would be Hell enough in itself. Yet let's be clear it is the choice of Man, in defiant and stubborn rebellion to his own source, not God's choice, but Man who refuses to the last to acknowledge his errors;

OH NO NOT JESUS

THE DEVIL HELL AND ALL THAT SCARY STUFF

ignoring the testimony within his own heart of the truth and
hardened to the call of God.

Timothy 2: 1-6
New International Version (NIV)

*I urge, then, first of all, that requests, prayers, intercession and
thanksgiving be made for everyone for kings and all those in
authority, that we may live peaceful and quiet lives in all godliness
and holiness. This is good, and pleases God our Saviour, who
wants all men to be saved and to come to a knowledge of the
truth. For there is one God and one mediator between God and
men, the man Christ Jesus, who gave himself as a ransom for all
men the testimony given in its proper time.*

2 Peter 3: 9
New International Version (NIV)

*The Lord is not slow in keeping his promise, as some understand
slowness. He is patient with you, not wanting anyone to perish,
but everyone to come to repentance.*

Of course, the answer to the equation and the alternative ending to
the narrative is to return home in the confidence that far from what
our worst best friend would have us believe, our Father will receive
us.

John 6: 37
New International Version (NIV)

*All those the Father gives me will come to me, and whoever comes
to me I will never drive away.*

A Loving God?

What real evidence is there that God is a loving God when for many the world more often than not seems to provide assurances to the contrary?

My pre-Jesus understanding of God (not that you would have heard me using that term) as an entity rather detached from everyday goings on, existing on some ethereal plain that through spiritual training we could obtain a return ticket to, had afforded this entirely fictional distant deity the luxury of deflecting basic questions about personal suffering and the collective chaos of Man's earthly existence. Following the encounters I described in the first chapter though, and as I continued to experience Jesus' guidance daily through the promptings of his spirit, the Bible and the ministering of his word, the fact that God was a personal God, had become undeniable.

What then was the answer to this familiar charge if it wasn't just that God simply "wasn't that involved"?

Catastrophic natural disasters, disease, inhumanly brutal wars, murder, corruption and injustice along with the rest of the world's heart breaking ills can lead many to believe that if God is personal, in the biblical numbering the hairs on our head sense, then surely our times are proof that God really has taken his eye off the ball! Or even, perhaps, this apparent perpetual suffering and conflict experienced by so many innocent people around the world is proof after all that there really is no God!

If not, then where is God in all this?

And:

Why isn't he doing anything about it all?

And:

What about natural disasters? If we are to believe that God made the world then surely these are a result of his faulty workmanship aren't they?

In the context of all of this, the idea of dire consequences awaiting us after it's all over should we, for the duration of our lives, have refused to acknowledge an unseen God can be, depending on where we are at, slightly bewildering.

What I am hoping to share with you in what follows, as you may by now expect, is that the answers for these very worthwhile questions can be found within the pages of his love letter to mankind. Again, I will require your brutal honesty and openness in sincere self-appraisal to surpass that which I could manage for a considerable amount of time, else I fully expect that there will be nothing to be gained from reading this chapter.

With the disclaimer in place, we'll continue.

As well as being a spiritual guide, the Bible, I discovered, is also a practical historical record of God's relationship with Man, from His inception to where we stand today. Looking at the Bible in this light we are able to gain an insight into the heart of God with regards to these matters. (For those who are unwilling to accept the authenticity of the Bible, the following chapter deals with this subject so either wait for that or allow yourself to entertain the notion that the Bible could be a reliable document until then).

On Wars and the Evils of Man

Undoubtedly the God of the Bible is a God of peace whose plan for mankind is to live at peace with his neighbour. To see mankind, created in the image of God to live wholly as Gods earthly representative, engaged in acts of violence against his fellow man must be one of the most obvious signs of his rebellion and fall.

The disobedience and rebellion of his father, Adam, and inherited by Cain bore the fruit of murder when Cain, through jealousy of his brother's standing with God, murders Abel. From then to the time of Noah things appear to have gone from bad to worse:

Genesis 6: 13
New International Version (NIV)

So God said to Noah, "I am going to put an end to all people, for the earth is filled with violence because of them. I am surely going to destroy both them and the earth".

The God of the Bible as well as being a God of peace is also a God of Justice. God as the creator and <u>author</u> of life here, unlike the situation with his handling of the Cain situation, whom he preserves from death, exercises his <u>author-ity</u> to end it!

Coming from my "all we need is love", law abiding middle England bubble it was hard to see how the prospect of a God who brought justice and judgement to the rebellious was a good thing. What I was really finding it hard to come to terms with was the idea of a God that would be wrathful where I would show mercy. In black and white it seems so obviously misguided. The God of the Bible is a God of divine patience, long suffering and mercy that sees all ends and always hopes long after we would have incinerated whole Continents.

Luke 9: 54-55
Amplified Bible (AMP)

And when His disciples James and John observed this, they said, Lord, do You wish us to command fire to come down from heaven and consume them, even as Elijah did?

But He turned and rebuked and severely censured them. He said, You do not know of what sort of spirit you are.

Just to reinforce the argument:

Ezekiel 18: 23
New International Version

Do I take pleasure in the death of the wicked? Declares the sovereign Lord. Rather, am I not pleased when they turn from their ways and live?

In Nineveh, the capital city of the Assyrians, where Jonah reluctantly preached, the people did just that, much to the annoyance of Jonah who, after all his troubles, was at least expecting a few volleys of fire and brimstone from heaven!

Violence was and is clearly the outward manifestation of degenerative culture that does not know or revere the God of the Bible. For the Israelites, as God's sole chosen vehicle through which to bring the nations to the knowledge of God (meaning also they were the sole regenerative society on the face of the earth), this meant that peace often had to be fought for.

Situated at the crossroads of the ancient world to be a witness to the nations, God would fulfil His promise of bringing them rest from the violence of the nations that surrounded them.

Deuteronomy 12: 10
New International Version (NIV)

But you will cross the Jordan and settle in the land the Lord your God is giving you as an inheritance, and he will give you rest from all your enemies around you so that you will live in safety.

Joshua 21: 44
New International Version (NIV)

The Lord gave them rest on every side, just as he had sworn to their ancestors, Not one of their enemies withstood them; the Lord gave all their enemies into their hands.

Under the faithful rule of David and Solomon, heeding the direction of God, they continued to triumph super-naturally over their aggressive neighbours, bringing about the desired end of such peace and prosperity that foreign dignitaries would visit to inquire into the source of their blessing.

Then, as Israel faltered in holding to the covenant that God had made with them, conflict within and without increased. The nation split in two before eventually being conquered by the Babylonians.

God tells them of a time, however, when the fight to restore peace on earth is taken to a new frontier and the source of all conflict is dealt with.

Isaiah 9: 5-7
New International Version (NIV)

Every warrior's boot used in battle
* and every garment rolled in blood*
will be destined for burning,
* will be fuel for the fire.*
For to us a child is born,
* to us a son is given,*
* and the government will be on his shoulders.*
And he will be called
* Wonderful Counselor, Mighty God,*
* Everlasting Father, Prince of Peace.*
Of the greatness of his government and peace
* there will be no end.*
He will reign on David's throne
* and over his kingdom,*
establishing and upholding it
* with justice and righteousness*
* from that time on and forever.*
The zeal of the Lord Almighty
* will accomplish this.*

This Prince of Peace would teach that all the laws of Moses could be summed up in the two commands, 'Love the Lord your God with all your heart and mind and all your strength' and 'love your neighbour as yourself'! A nation of individual agents of regeneration from within a variety of world cultures would now work with God to bring nations the mercy and knowledge of God.

Clearly God's desire is for peace on earth. It is also clear that in the past, direct intervention has been employed to secure it. So seeing that the world appears to be in a perpetual state of conflict with nations groaning in anguish, the question naturally arises; why then has God not stopped the show a long time ago, enforced his rule and saved the earth the suffering and the bloodshed?

Well this is one of the quickest answers I'm sure I will give in these writings so blink and you'll miss it. Because the good news, as far as the Bible is concerned, is that God is apparently in agreement with us about the state of the world. On coming down and sorting it all out the answer is yes too, this is exactly what he has promised to do. The time and date of this event, however, we have to leave to his superior judgement, as it is he who stands outside of time and sees all ends.

And it gets better... Revelation, the final book of the Bible, tells us that God will return our loved ones that have died to new life and create a new universe and a new earth where he will dwell with us and wipe away every tear from our eyes. There will be no more death or mourning and He will bring to realisation the hope of a world free from evil which will all begin with the return, in power this time, of His Son, Jesus Christ, riding on the clouds.

Hopefully this short answer makes a refreshing change. The next obvious question which may need more explaining is:

When?

Famously, we don't know. We are given indicators of the sort of place the world will be when this event occurs but we are expressly told that we will never be given a specific date.

Matthew 24: 36-39
New International Version (NIV)

"But about that day or hour no one knows, not even the angels in heaven, nor the Son, but only the Father. As it was in the days of Noah, so it will be at the coming of the Son of Man. For in the days before the flood, people were eating and drinking, marrying and giving in marriage, up to the day Noah entered the ark; and they knew nothing about what would happen until the flood came and took them all away. That is how it will be at the coming of the Son of Man."

2 Timothy 3: 1-5
New International Version (NIV)

"But mark this: There will be terrible times in the last days. People will be lovers of themselves, lovers of money, boastful, proud, abusive, disobedient to their parents, ungrateful, unholy, without love, unforgiving, slanderous, without self-control, brutal, not lovers of the good, treacherous, rash, conceited, lovers of pleasure rather than lovers of God—having a form of godliness but denying its power. Have nothing to do with such people".

Although this last scripture mentions the "last days" and lists some frighteningly familiar cultural characteristics, it's clear from the letters of the early church leaders in the New Testament that they lived in daily anticipation of the return of their Lord. So seeing as it's been 2000 years or so now are we allowed to ask:

Where is he?

Echoing psalm ninety, Peter reminds us that God has a different perspective of time than we do, and rather than tut-tutting and tapping our wrists we ought to be grateful and full of adoration for his patience.

2 Peter 3: 8-9
New International Version (NIV)

"But do not forget this one thing, dear friends. With the Lord a day is like a thousand years and a thousand years are like a day. The Lord is not slow in keeping his promise, as some understand slowness. Instead he is patient with you, not wanting anyone to perish, but everyone to come to repentance".

If there is any delay then we are assured it is for our benefit. Because item number one on God's agenda, and the focal point of the book of the history of his relationship with Man, is the battle to regain the affections of His wayward special creation, from the entity that encouraged his rebellion and now holds him captive.

Matthew 13: 24-43
New International Version (NIV)

Jesus told them another parable: "The kingdom of heaven is like a man who sowed good seed in his field. But while everyone was sleeping, his enemy came and sowed weeds among the wheat, and went away. When the wheat sprouted and formed heads, then the weeds also appeared.

"The owner's servants came to him and said, 'Sir, didn't you sow good seed in your field? Where then did the weeds come from?'

"'An enemy did this,' he replied.

"The servants asked him, 'Do you want us to go and pull them up?'

"'No,' he answered, 'because while you are pulling the weeds, you may uproot the wheat with them. Let both grow together until the harvest. At that time I will tell the harvesters: First collect the weeds and tie them in bundles to be burned; then gather the wheat and bring it into my barn.'"

We are assured by the life of Jesus that God is in no ways disconnected or distant from our troubles in this life. He has himself experienced and shared in the suffering of this world in the person of Jesus Christ, King of Israel, tortured, killed, spat upon and mocked unjustly at the demand of the very people he had come to save. He suffered with those who suffer; he was treated unjustly with those who have never known justice; he was reviled by those he loved and he undeservedly met with death himself like so many. If we want to know where God is amongst all the suffering of the innocent, he is right there with those that suffer.

God doesn't offer excuses or complex philosophy for the state of the world. He offers us an explanation, a solution and the promise of justice for the persecuted, the innocent and the poor, and a future hope of a world free from the influence of evil that will endure forever. While he works we are asked to remain patient.

Revelation 13: 10
New International Version (NIV)

"If anyone is to go into captivity,
  into captivity they will go.
If anyone is to be killed with the sword,
  with the sword they will be killed."

This calls for patient endurance and faithfulness on the part of God's people.

The door to our freedom, where the separation from God and the captivity of our accuser is ended and eternity begins, stands open today. With only the return of Jesus Christ to bring a close to current proceedings, the death of Jesus Christ makes our spiritual generation the last of this age of creation. All that is required of us is that we accept God's gift of salvation, metaphorically walking through the open door set before us. Yet though we are now one step away from heaven, the very fact that heaven is so accessible by nature increases our culpability should we choose not to take that step.

John 3: 19
New International Version (NIV)

This is the verdict: Light has come into the world, but people loved darkness instead of light because their deeds were evil.

The Bible is resolute in its message that God has made His intentions clear and accessible to all and has made His desire for us to believe in His Son known. He has given more than enough and all He is going to give: the ball is now in our court.

Yet often we are so reviled by and suspicious of any talk about the existence of evil and unprepared to entertain talk of the issues with Man that the Garden of Eden narrative represents that the Divine judgement side of this resolution to the world's ills often forms an ironic catch twenty two argument against the Gospel when we only possess a vague understanding of its message. In that it is not uncommon for us (I am assuming that I am not alone in this) that after bringing down the shutters on any talk of evil, that in the next breath we hold God responsible, or at least guilty of gross negligence, with regards to mass pain and suffering. Our role, of course, in all this is as innocent bystanders. (Mmm, starting to sound familiar...) Then on receiving the news that God has promised to bring about a sudden change to this age of corruption and pronounce a final holy Judgement that will once and for all time separate that which is wholeheartedly dedicated to evil from that which is truly good, our response is to be duly justified in our suspicion that, if this dubious deity is anything like that which was made in his image, he is more than likely going to send huge swathes of people to a lake of fire who never really deserved it!

In a nutshell, we don't trust him!

(Now we are on familiar ground again)

What we are failing to acknowledge in this reasoning, like Adam, is the true character of God. That although we are made in His image, his character ought not to be brought into question by our own failure to heed His very direction. What we ought to be questioning is what illnesses would the world still have if Man were to truly and wholeheartedly dedicate himself to God.

Isaiah 55: 9
New International Version (NIV)

As the heavens are higher than the earth, so are my ways higher than your ways and my thoughts than your thoughts.

If man were to truly "Love God with all his heart" and "Love his neighbour as himself" then surely there would be no war, and that would leave time and resources to deal with any other natural problems. But it seems our complaint is that God won't take control, yet one of our most common complaints is that this teaching seeks to control us! We can't have it both ways, although it seems we always have had the same problem:

Matthew 11: 16-19
New International Version (NIV)

To what can I compare this generation? They are like children sitting in the marketplaces and calling out to others

"'We played the pipe for you,
*   and you did not dance;*
we sang a dirge,
*   and you did not mourn.'*

For John came neither eating nor drinking, and they say, 'He has a demon.' The Son of Man came eating and drinking, and they say, 'Here is a glutton and a drunkard, a friend of tax collectors and sinners.' But wisdom is proved right by her deeds.

We are failing in our assessment of this prophesied last event of the age to appreciate the perfection of our Father's intents: His perfect love for mankind and that His judgements are not based on flawed human knowledge but on the boundless knowledge that knew us before it began to knit us together in our mother's womb, and that sees the depths of our hearts; whose perfect love and plan for us was expressed in and through the life of Jesus Christ.

To understand and have respect for the passages of the Bible which speak of God's justice we must first know the God whose "grace and mercy endures forever" and grant Him the proper reverence He warrants. In other words we must acknowledge that the God of the Bible is a Holy God. Yet as we are culturally becoming increasingly estranged from the reality of the joy that salvation brings, the very idea of holiness becomes an offence to many in a popular culture where acceptance of a life of compromise and powerlessness permeates every arena. In place of sermons encouraging us to fight the good fight of faith; we have monologues from sharp tongued comedians, who know no bounds to ridicule and hold nothing as sacred, to reassure us of the deceptiveness of high ideals.

But if we can lay aside this for a moment and allow ourselves to believe that there is something untainted still in this life that is worthy of our attention then we can maybe start to consider what holiness means.

Higher than the highest concepts of the human mind and the deepest longing of the human heart, it is spiritual purity that, when encountered, can inspire a combination of fear, awe or even great distress that even the most dedicated of men are overwhelmed.

Here are a few examples of this from scripture:

Adam: We have already discussed, who having willingly gone against God hid from God's presence.

Moses: After escaping from Pharaoh's army the Israelites at the

foot of the mountain where Moses received the Ten
Commandments, begged Moses to bring God's word to them
himself rather than have God speak to them directly. Such was the
terror in their hearts on encountering the voice of God.

Exodus 20:18-19
New International Version (NIV)

*When the people saw the thunder and lightning and heard the
trumpet and saw the mountain in smoke, they trembled with
fear. They stayed at a distance and said to Moses, "Speak to us
yourself and we will listen. But do not have God speak to us or we
will die."*

Later on in the life of Moses, when he asked to see God as he is, he
was told he would only be allowed to see His back as He passed by
as no man could see God and live!

Exodus 33: 18-20
Amplified Bible (AMP)

And Moses said, I beseech You, show me Your glory.

*And God said, I will make all My goodness pass before you, and I
will proclaim My name, The Lord, before you; for I will be gracious
to whom I will be gracious, and will show mercy and loving-
kindness on whom I will show mercy and loving-kindness.*

*But, He said, You can not see My face, for no man shall see Me and
live.*

Isaiah, on encountering a vision of God said:

Isaiah 6: 5
New International Version (NIV)

*"Woe to me!" I cried. "I am ruined! For I am a man of unclean
lips, and I live among a people of unclean lips, and my eyes have*

seen the King, the Lord Almighty."

Ezekiel:

Ezekiel 1:27-28
New International Version (NIV)

I saw that from what appeared to be his waist up he looked like glowing metal, as if full of fire, and that from there down he looked like fire; and brilliant light surrounded him. Like the appearance of a rainbow in the clouds on a rainy day, so was the radiance around him. This was the appearance of the likeness of the glory of the Lord. When I saw it, I fell facedown, and I heard the voice of one speaking.

Daniel, on encountering a vision of God:

Daniel 10: 15-17
New International Version (NIV)

While he was saying this to me, I bowed with my face toward the ground and was speechless. Then one who looked like a man touched my lips, and I opened my mouth and began to speak. I said to the one standing before me, "I am overcome with anguish because of the vision, my lord, and I feel very weak. How can I, your servant, talk with you, my lord? My strength is gone and I can hardly breathe."

Revelation 6:16
New International Version (NIV)

They called to the mountains and the rocks, "Fall on us and hide us from the face of him who sits on the throne and from the wrath of the Lamb!"

In God's presence things are what they are and there is no escaping it. God is Holy and we are unworthy on our own merit to partner with him in anything, yet clothed in the covering of Jesus the response is quite different.

God's focus is on our eternity with him, that we should not meet him without having first met with and accepted the offer of this covering provided by Jesus Christ through his death. Referring back to the question of 'Where is he?', His delay, far from being seen as evidence of His disregard for His creation, when correctly understood is evidence of His divine patience, long suffering and mercy.

In all that has been discussed, it is our attitude or opinion of God that colours how we take any of it and the crux of the whole matter in the end. I have arranged and re-arranged the paragraphs to try and put the arguments in an agreeable sequence, yet if we have no reason to warrant God with more respect than any stranger we might meet on the street, the sequence is unimportant. Our God underpins the whole of creation moment by moment and is worth more than the benefit of doubt, and instead is worth true reverence and awe.

Natural Disasters and the Angry Planet

Understanding man as a wayward part of God's creation under spiritual captivity to God's enemies, we can at least build a framework to explain the evils of mankind against his fellow being. But how then do we approach suffering that mankind seemingly has no involvement in: Earthquakes, Tsunamis, Hurricanes, Volcanoes erupting and the like.

This is one of those questions that a believing person can't ever provide a satisfactory answer to the unbelieving mind as the reassurance the believer gains with regards to these horrific occurrences is in the main part related to the understanding and experience of the person of God and His character or more specifically His care for individuals. However we will attempt to outline some of the main themes of scripture.

In the biblical scheme of things, mankind is intrinsically linked with his environment. Genesis tells us that we were formed from the earth and that the earth is given to us to care for whilst in return it would provide us with all the food we require. But as a result of Adam's rebellion he is told that the land, from which he was made, shall be cursed and be a curse to him.

Later when Cain murders Abel, God asks Cain why his murdered brother's blood cries out to him from the earth.

Factor in the scripture below and we get a picture of the earth in scripture as a suffering entity under the rule of rebellious Man who is neglecting his role as its chief caretaker but sharing the anticipation of a day of redemption with mankind.

Romans 8: 18-25
New International Version (NIV)

I consider that our present sufferings are not worth comparing with the glory that will be revealed in us. The creation waits in eager expectation for the sons of God to be revealed. For the creation was subjected to frustration, not by its own choice, but by the will of the one who subjected it, in hope that the creation itself will be liberated from its bondage to decay and brought into the glorious freedom of the children of God.

We know that the whole creation has been groaning as in the pains of childbirth right up to the present time. Not only so, but we ourselves, who have the first fruits of the Spirit, groan inwardly as we wait eagerly for our adoption as sons, the redemption of our bodies. For in this hope we were saved. But hope that is seen is no hope at all. Who hopes for what he already has? But if we hope for what we do not yet have, we wait for it patiently.

Far from ascending to a higher plane amongst the clouds somewhere, the biblical plan for the future age sets Man fulfilling his original purpose as God's representative and caretaker of a renewed earth in the absence of our old worst best friend. Where Isaiah tells us that: "the Lion will lay down with the Lamb and the child shall play by the cobra's nest". The redemption of man will also be the redemption of the creation too.

In Bible terms, since the coming of Jesus we have been a world in transition also sometimes referred to as the overlapping of the ages where the, ever spiritually increasing, coming kingdom of God advances towards its physical fulfilment and the passing age crashes and burns to its physical and spiritual deadline, trying to cause as much damage as possible on its way out. The closer we get to the deadline, the more intense the forces at play become.

Revelation 12: 12
New International Version (NIV)

Therefore rejoice, you heavens
  and you who dwell in them!
But woe to the earth and the sea,
  because the devil has gone down to you!
He is filled with fury,
  because he knows that his time is short.

Also Jesus himself offers this explanation repeated in Matthew, Mark and Luke's Gospels:

Mark 13: 5-8
New International Version (NIV)

Jesus said to them: "Watch out that no one deceives you. Many will come in my name, claiming, 'I am he,' and will deceive many. When you hear of wars and rumours of wars, do not be alarmed. Such things must happen, but the end is still to come. Nation will rise against nation and kingdom against kingdom. There will be earthquakes in various places, and famines. These are the beginning of birth pains.

Jesus does not mince His words here and is clear that as the age of Man comes to an end the ever intensifying spiritual battle will be echoed by the earth as creation becomes more tumultuous the closer we get to Jesus' return, a statement which is backed up by modern day scientific monitoring of natural disasters.

'Phew!', you might be thinking, 'at least he didn't say that natural disasters were the hand of God!'

Well no I didn't, we are saying that Man's fall from grace has impacted his environment and far from being the caretaker of the earth Man, in line with his fallen nature, has in many instances become the exploiter and destructor of God's creation. For example: the burning of fossil fuels, resulting in the dawning reality of future generations being saddled with an irrevocably damaged planet.

However, and this is the point where we are going to have to be one hundred percent honest with ourselves with regards to human nature, the final book of the Bible foretells of a time of terrible natural calamities as part of the final act of God's redemptive plan for mankind.

Before anyone spits, please continue.

We have talked about the rebellion of human heart towards God and I hope I have managed to present adequately in the previous chapters the biblical understanding of the role Man's free will has within creation and also that it is not God's will for anyone to be separated from Him after this life is over but for all to turn away from their inherited rebellion and accept his offer of restoration.

If we accept that this is God's overwhelming desire for humanity as a whole, of which the crucifixion of his Son was a graphic display, then we must ask how is God going to go about making sure that everyone who can possibly be won over for God is won over. Surely we don't expect God just to be random about what day he chooses to usher in the renewed creation. There must be a plan.

Well there is a plan in action right now which we are a part of, we'll get to this later, but when it gets to five to midnight how is God going to ensure that every last soul is saved? So the question put another way is… What circumstances are going to be conducive to a wholesale seeking of God in humility and repentance by all of mankind before the last grains of the sands of time fall?

Should it start raining fifty pound notes?

Or maybe we could all be given the ability to fly without assistance?

Would these or any other form of material or physical blessing result in wholesale change of heart towards our creator?

Well in terms of blessing, many of us have more than enough. God has provided the rains to come in season and the land yields its fruit. Often our human systems fail us by creating poverty and need where there needn't be, as there really is enough to go around. In terms of God's provision for even the massive populations of today we can have no complaints. In spite of this, our daily lives too often become all consuming and taking time out to be thankful for all we have becomes a foreign notion. Oftentimes it is only when some event with negative consequences directly impacts our daily lives that we stop to consider the bigger picture with solemnity.

God desires that even the most rebellious of people return to him. But the hard, cold truth is that hardened rebellious Man is not going to reconsider his standpoint toward God by a million pounds being deposited in his bank account by Bank of God plc, or any other material blessing. The acts of God that we are told shall accompany the final days of the current age will be a clear display of the power of God in seven intensifying stages, in order that the people of that dark time may be afforded the opportunity, to reposition themselves before the return of Jesus Christ and the end of the age.

Revelation 21: 1-4
New International Version (NIV)

A New Heaven and a New Earth

Then I saw "a new heaven and a new earth," for the first heaven and the first earth had passed away, and there was no longer any sea. I saw the Holy City, the new Jerusalem, coming down out of heaven from God, prepared as a bride beautifully dressed for her husband. And I heard a loud voice from the throne saying, "Look! God's dwelling place is now among the people, and he will dwell with them. They will be his people, and God himself will be with them and be their God. 'He will wipe every tear from their eyes. There will be no more death' or mourning or crying or pain, for the old order of things has passed away."

The Authenticity of the Bible

Undoubtedly, you will have noticed that to this point I have quoted from various translations of the Bible extensively without any question of its reliability, in terms of it being an accurate record of the events and sayings of its main characters. But how do we know that these writings are reliable? What evidence do we have that these are the true writings of the followers of Jesus and how can we be sure that they have not been doctored or altered by unscrupulous men seeking to promote their own version of the teachings of Jesus based around personal or social prejudices ,or social/political aims?

Aren't there other writings and other Gospels? If so, who decided what got into the Bible and what didn't? Is the Church censoring the real Jesus?

Well for my part, following accepting Jesus at the New Testament Church of God in Leeds, the Bible, which had previously been one of those books that I had been unable to pick up, as I described earlier, suddenly became alive like no other book I had ever read and remains thus to this day. In itself, this was enough to convince me of its spiritual validity, nevertheless the research that I share in this chapter was a comfort and an encouragement in the face of popular recurring aspersions cast against this most notorious of documents. Hopefully, if the historical validity and authenticity of these writings is a major obstacle to taking the claims of the Bible seriously then this chapter will be for you.

Exhibit A: Jesus and his teaching exist historically outside of the Bible, as do the behaviours and beliefs of his followers recorded by first century Roman and Jewish historians. E.g., the first century Roman historian Suetonius, chief secretary to Emperor Hadrian, wrote that there was a man named Chrestus (or Christ) who lived during the first century (*Annals* 15.44).

Unfortunately also for those who love a good conspiracy theory and despite the hype of recent popular culture (Dan Brown and all the rest of it), any serious investigation into the authenticity and reliability of the Bible texts has always returned the same verdict: that the ancient writings that our modern day Bibles are translated from are found to be the most reliable and error free of any ancient writings by a good country mile. This is by virtue of the sheer volume of manuscript evidence discovered as compared to other ancient writings, the variety of locations in which the manuscripts were found, Egypt, Palestine, Syria, Turkey, Greece, and Italy, thus making collusion unlikely, and also in terms of the amount of time between the events described and the date of the document. See below:

Manuscript Evidence for Ancient Writings				
Author	Written	Earliest Copy	Time Span	# Mss.
Caesar	100-44 B.C.	900 A.D.	1,000 yrs	10
Plato	427-347 B.C.	900 A.D.	1,200 yrs	7
Thucydides	460-400 B.C.	900 A.D.	1,300 yrs	8
Tacitus	100 A.D.	1100 A.D.	1,000 yrs	20
Suetonius	75-160 A.D.	950 A.D.	800 yrs	8
Homer (Iliad)	900 B.C.	400 B.C.	500 yrs	643
New Testament	40-100 A.D.	125 A.D.	25-50 yrs	24,000

The oldest New Testament manuscript, the John Rylands

manuscript, has been dated to 125 A.D. and was found in Egypt, some distance from where the New Testament was originally composed in Asia Minor. Many early Christian papyri, discovered in 1935, have been dated to 150 A.D., and include the four Gospels. The Papyrus Bodmer II, discovered in 1956, has been dated to 200 A.D., and contains 14 chapters and portions of the last seven chapters of the Gospel of John. The Chester Beatty biblical papyri, discovered in 1931, has been dated to 200-250 A.D. and contains the Gospels, Acts, Paul's Epistles, and Revelation.

Sir William Ramsey, a notable archaeologist of his time, had, prior to his archaeological research at the turn of the century in Asia, believed that the writings of Luke which consist of the Gospel that bears his name and the book of Acts, the 'what the Disciples did next book', were totally unreliable.

However, following extensive excavations in Asia Minor, Ramsay made many discoveries which actually proved the historical reliability of Luke's writings to such a degree that Ramsey's own scepticism of the texts, and therefore of the faith, were cast aside and Ramsey became a believer, concluding:

> "Luke is a historian of the first rank; not merely are his statements of fact trustworthy; he is possessed of the true historic sense; he fixes his mind on the idea and plan that rules in the evolution of history; and proportions the scale of his treatment to the importance of each incident." (*The Bearing of Recent Discovery on the Trustworthiness of the New Testament.* Sir W M Ramsey) (Public Domain)

Luke's accuracy in his use of titles throughout his writings has been verified as correct, in some instances by archaeological discoveries within the last century. This in itself is no mean feat as Roman titles were constantly changing and Luke wasn't afforded the luxury of a local library for his research.

Speaking generally now with regards to the New Testament it

seems that somewhere along the line many of us, in which I include myself, have been given the impression of there being an unexplained void in Church history, a kind of historical black hole, in which it could have been possible that anything could have happened to these writings and out of which emerged this assembly of writings we now call the Bible.

In fact with just a little research it's easy to discover that there is no such historical void and that the timeline of the organisation known as the Church, from the time of the protégés of the Disciples, such as Ignatius, student of John and Bishop of Antioch born 35 AD - died 108 AD, quoting John 3:8 in his writings, to the invention of the printing press is unbroken.

What is known as the canonisation of the books of the New Testament, that is the decisions about which writings to use and which not to use, wasn't simply a random concoction of what were thought to be the best but was a reaction to the emergence of many manuscripts of dubious authenticity emerging in the second century, popularly known as Gnostic writings.

These writings, although considered useful by the early Church, were not included in the cannon due to the fact that they could not be verified as being from first century, or first generation, Christian sources.

As for the Old Testament and its own authenticity, we have the Dead Sea Scrolls, discovered between 1947 and 1956, dating back to the time of Christ which contain two exact copies of Isaiah and segments of every book from the Old Testament, except Esther, with only minor differences found, the most notable of which refer to names and places within the book of Daniel, not something which would cause a wholesale re-evaluation of our faith.

The same can be said of textural inconsistencies within the Gospels. For example, critics will point to inconsistencies with the order of events between the Gospels, which critics seek to exploit to prove the fallibility of the Bible. Such critics, I would advise, seem to have really missed the point (it seems) of what the Gospel authors were commissioned to do. In that, although providing an accurate account of the sequence of events had some bearing on the output of the Gospel authors, we can be certain that this wasn't their primary aim. Their primary purpose was, lest we should forget, to communicate the teachings and life of Jesus Christ as displayed through his words and actions, culminating in his death and resurrection and how he was the fulfilment of Old Testament prophesies of the coming Messiah.

In this task, generations have attested to the fact that they have more than excelled. Although timelines of events may differ ever so slightly, the person and acts of Jesus Christ are recorded sufficiently that we may know that each Gospel speaks clearly of the same person with the same teachings.

Often because the Bible is described as the Word of God, it is thought that Christians believe that God dictated the entire Bible word by word to the author. In some instances this is true, for example the Ten Commandments and the Law of Moses. But in other portions of scripture, the inspiration of the writer comes from God as the Holy Spirit guides and enables him to see the mind and heart of God as he utilises his individual gifts and personality in the written expression. For example, in the aforementioned case of Luke, the author's apparent gift for meticulous attention to detail in the recording of names and titles of important figures of the time has become invaluable.

Does this involvement of man make these writings therefore less divine? No, in this we have an example of Man fulfilling his original purpose as God's earthly representative and steward over his creation. Man and God labouring together in the garden. This is what Jesus calls each of us too, when he invites us to take his yoke upon us:

Matthew 11: 29
New International Version (NIV)

"Take my yoke upon you and learn from me, for I am gentle and humble in heart, and you will find rest for your souls..."

It's nothing to do with eggs, as I thought for far too long: a yoke is a harness for a pair of animals or labourers to pull. Jesus said my burden is light and my yoke is easy. We are designed to live in relationship and work in partnership with God. The men of the Bible weren't perfect, however they were in relationship with, inspired by, chosen by and obedient to the calling of the God, who is perfect, upon their lives.

The result is a book with 40 different authors of varying intellect and social standing over a period of 1500 years, written before the age of telecommunications or printing presses, containing 66 volumes in several different languages that speak consistently of the same creator God with the same character and purpose.

Returning to the central theme and the whole point of the matter rather than be distracted by what amounts to as much as a missing comma here and an absent full stop there... as a spiritual guide then, inspired by God, written by people chosen for the job by God, for the needs of mankind and the answers to the biggest questions, the Bible is indeed the perfect book. If there are those who are prepared to disregard it due to proof reading errors then unfortunately they are really missing the point and are most likely willingly avoiding seeing the wood for the trees. This summation at the end of John's Gospel could easily be applied to the whole Bible:

John 21: 25
New International Version (NIV)

Jesus did many other things as well. If every one of them were written down, I suppose that even the whole world would not have room for the books that would be written.

In other words 'I could go on but this is enough'. The Bible itself is complete, up to date, relevant and fit for purpose. Our job, which is one of utmost importance, is to understand the narrative that runs through it and how it relates to our situation.

"A thorough understanding of the BIBLE is better than a college education"

(Theodore Roosevelt)

Prophesy

Let's look now at this question from another angle. We have addressed the historical and textural questions about this world all time best seller but there is another aspect of these writings which make the Bible like no other book, which you would probably be best to ignore if you're trying to maintain the position of disregarding the Bible as the fantastical writings of over-imaginative men.

That is the question of prophesies found within it. The Bible is full of them which relate to past, present and future events, the most famous of which is surely the foretold return of Jesus Christ.

So why should we believe any of these and is there any proof that any such proclamations have ever been fulfilled?

Put simply, yes, and unfortunately far too many to go into all of them, books have been written that are solely devoted to the subject. So I'll just provide a handful of varied Bible prophesies to give you a taste of the subject.

Genesis 3: 15
New International Version (NIV)

 "... And I will put enmity
  between you and the woman,
  and between your offspring and hers;

he will crush your head,
and you will strike his heel."

Perhaps a bit mystical for some readers but nevertheless one of the most famous, this passage is God addressing the devil in the Garden of Eden shortly after the rebellion of Adam and Eve. The seed of the serpent is those who follow the teachings of the serpent and rebel against God. The seed of the woman, ultimately, speaks of Jesus who figuratively crushed the serpent's head or, non-figuratively, disempowered the accuser of our conscience and our personal spiritual, psychological and emotional jailer.

Jeremiah 32: 32-42
New International Version (NIV)

"The people of Israel and Judah have provoked me by all the evil they have done—they, their kings and officials, their priests and prophets, the people of Judah and those living in Jerusalem. They turned their backs to me and not their faces; though I taught them again and again, they would not listen or respond to discipline. They set up their vile images in the house that bears my Name and defiled it. They built high places for Baal in the Valley of Ben Hinnom to sacrifice their sons and daughters to Molek, though I never commanded—nor did it enter my mind — that they should do such a detestable thing and so make Judah sin.

"You are saying about this city, 'By the sword, famine and plague it will be given into the hands of the king of Babylon'; but this is what the Lord, the God of Israel, says: I will surely gather them from all the lands where I banish them in my furious anger and great wrath; I will bring them back to this place and let them live in safety. They will be my people, and I will be their God. I will give them singleness of heart and action, so that they will always fear me and that all will then go well for them and for their children after them. I will make an everlasting covenant with them: I will never stop doing good to them, and I will inspire them

*to fear me, so that they will never turn away from me. I will
rejoice in doing them good and will assuredly plant them in this
land with all my heart and soul.*

*"This is what the Lord says: As I have brought all this great
calamity on this people, so I will give them all the prosperity I have
promised them."*

The prophet Jeremiah, here speaking as a mouthpiece for God, tells
the people of Israel, in no uncertain terms, of their fate. After
overthrowing the Assyrian empire, the Babylonians destroyed
Jerusalem and the temple in 586 B.C. Following the toppling of the
Babylonians by the Medo-Persians under Cyrus the Great,
Jerusalem began to be rebuilt. The second temple being completed
70 years after the Israelites were taken into captivity.

Jeremiah 50: 38-39
New International Version (NIV)

*"A drought on her waters!
    They will dry up.
For it is a land of idols,
    idols that will go mad with terror."*

*"So desert creatures and hyenas will live there,
    and there the owl will dwell.
It will never again be inhabited
    or lived in from generation to generation."*

The nation of Israel was disciplined through their exile for all of
their wrong doing. But disciplined is not forsaken and when, after a
time, the hearts of the Jewish people returned to their God and
their God returned to them, God's attention turned to their captors:

Babylon was the great man-made institution of the ancient world;
being the first city to have a population exceeding 200,000 it is
often thought of as the first real city. The 196 square miles of

Babylon were surrounded by 14 miles of 187ft thick 200ft high walls and her towers extended a further 100ft above the walls.

In the fourth century, however, the walls were completely destroyed by the Romans and the Euphrates River, which once flowed close to the city, has now moved nine miles west. Attempts to rebuild the city by Alexander the Great, and more recently Sadam Hussein, have been unsuccessful and quickly followed by their instigators' demise.

Ezekiel 26: 12
New International Version (NIV)

They will plunder your wealth and loot your merchandise; they will break down your walls and demolish your fine houses and throw your stones, timber and rubble into the sea.

The prophesy of Ezekiel here is against the city of Tyre, which was a strategically important harbour city located on an island a short distance from the mainland and as such gained great wealth. Like Babylon, Tyre was renowned for its heavy fortifications. A friend of Israel in the times of David and Solomon, the city is accused of a lack of loyalty towards its friend and of gloating over its destruction.

As with Babylon, the city mistook the act of God disciplining his chosen people for him forsaking them. As the people of Israel return to their God and him to them, God promises to restore their standing amongst their peers.

Such was the impenetrability of this fortress even the great Babylonian King Nebuchadnezzar, after 13 years of attacking the city, only managed to broker a deal whereby Tyre paid taxes to Babylon. It wasn't until Alexander the Great that this fortress was finally taken and the prophesy fulfilled. With very little land existing outside of the walls of this island fortress, its strength lay in the fact that the usual method of bringing siege towers against the walls of the city could not be employed. Or could it?

After various other methods had been exhausted, Alexander the Great used materials from the settlements on the shore to build a causeway between the mainland and the city where the water was only 18ft deep, thus enabling him to raise his siege works and take the city. So angered was Alexander by the amount of time wasted on this one city, he gave the order that the city was to be sacked without mercy. The causeway that Alexander built has now become a permanent feature making Tyre no longer an island.

Daniel 2: 31-45
New International Version (NIV)

"Your Majesty looked, and there before you stood a large statue— an enormous, dazzling statue, awesome in appearance. The head of the statue was made of pure gold, its chest and arms of silver, its belly and thighs of bronze, its legs of iron, its feet partly of iron and partly of baked clay. While you were watching, a rock was cut out, but not by human hands. It struck the statue on its feet of iron and clay and smashed them. Then the iron, the clay, the bronze, the silver and the gold were all broken to pieces and became like chaff on a threshing floor in the summer. The wind swept them away without leaving a trace. But the rock that struck the statue became a huge mountain and filled the whole earth.

"This was the dream, and now we will interpret it to the king. Your Majesty, you are the king of kings. The God of heaven has given you dominion and power and might and glory; in your hands he has placed all mankind and the beasts of the field and the birds in the sky. Wherever they live, he has made you ruler over them all. You are that head of gold.

"After you, another kingdom will arise, inferior to yours. Next, a third kingdom, one of bronze, will rule over the whole earth. Finally, there will be a fourth kingdom, strong as iron—for iron breaks and smashes everything—and as iron breaks things to pieces, so it will crush and break all the others. Just as you saw that the feet and toes were partly of baked clay and partly of iron,

so this will be a divided kingdom; yet it will have some of the strength of iron in it, even as you saw iron mixed with clay. As the toes were partly iron and partly clay, so this kingdom will be partly strong and partly brittle. And just as you saw the iron mixed with baked clay, so the people will be a mixture and will not remain united, any more than iron mixes with clay.

"In the time of those kings, the God of heaven will set up a kingdom that will never be destroyed, nor will it be left to another people. It will crush all those kingdoms and bring them to an end, but it will itself endure forever. This is the meaning of the vision of the rock cut out of a mountain, but not by human hands —a rock that broke the iron, the bronze, the clay, the silver and the gold to pieces.

"The great God has shown the king what will take place in the future. The dream is true and its interpretation is trustworthy."

The book of Daniel contains many famous fulfilled prophesies, of which this is just one example. This prophesy consists really of the whole chapter but the preceding excerpt will give us an outline of the subject.

The story goes that the mighty King Nebuchadnezzar of Babylon has a dream that terrifies him so much that he demands an authoritative explanation. Such is his desire to be sure that the interpretation is genuine, he refuses to tell anyone the particulars of the dream, and until someone is able meet his demand for an interpretation then his courtiers and sorcerers are to be murdered one by one.

His court are at a loss to know what to do and plead with the King, informing him that what he is asking is impossible and something that only God could know! Daniel, one of the captured Jews, having sought God in prayer with regards to the dream and its meaning presents his findings.

The following discourse, where Daniel shares with the King what God revealed to him, perfectly describes the kingdoms/empires that followed the Babylonian empire.

The kingdom of two arms of silver refers to the coalition of the Midianites and Persians which were soon to conquer Babylon.

The next kingdom, represented by the body of bronze, represents the great Grecian Empire under Alexander the Great which in turn was conquered by the Romans whose kingdom was divided into ten separate kingdoms of varying strength and are represented by the feet of clay and iron.

The final kingdom is the kingdom of God, established through Jesus Christ, whose sons and daughters, as described in the first chapter of John's Gospel, will be "children born not of natural descent, nor of human decision or a husband's will, but born of God".

In addition to this prophesy, the seventh chapter repeats the references to these kingdoms, albeit using different metaphor. The eleventh chapter goes on to described in great detail the political manoeuvrings of the forces occupying and surrounding Israel over four centuries which, although fascinating, I fear would be too much to go in to now.

Isaiah 7: 13-14
New International Version (NIV)

Then Isaiah said, "Hear now, you house of David! Is it not enough to try the patience of humans? Will you try the patience of my God also? Therefore the Lord himself will give you a sign: The virgin will conceive and give birth to a son, and will call him Immanuel."

Here, seven hundred years before the birth of Jesus, we have the nature of Jesus' birth described. Immanuel means God with us! Also note that the prophesy is directed to the house of David of which

Mary was a descendant.

Micah 5: 2
New International Version (NIV)

But you, Bethlehem Ephrathah, though you are small among the clans of Judah, out of you will come for me one who will be ruler over Israel, whose origins are from of old, from ancient times.

The appointed birthplace of the forthcoming messiah was well known to the educated Jewish community, so much so that although amazed by his words, the crowds who heard Jesus speak in the temple were hesitant to accept him on the basis of his presumed birthplace.

John 7: 40-42
New International Version (NIV)

On hearing his words, some of the people said, "Surely this man is the Prophet."

Others said, "He is the Messiah."

Still others asked, "How can the Messiah come from Galilee? Does not Scripture say that the Messiah will come from David's descendants and from Bethlehem, the town where David lived?"

Some of the most compelling prophesies are those which provided intimate detail of the character of Jesus and his ministry:

Isaiah 53: 2-9
New International Version (NIV)

He grew up before him like a tender shoot,
and like a root out of dry ground.
He had no beauty or majesty to attract us to him,
nothing in his appearance that we should desire him.

He was despised and rejected by men,
  a man of sorrows, and familiar with suffering.
  Like one from whom men hide their faces
  he was despised, and we esteemed him not.

Surely he took up our infirmities
  and carried our sorrows,
  yet we considered him stricken by God,
  smitten by him, and afflicted.

But he was pierced for our transgressions,
  he was crushed for our iniquities;
  the punishment that brought us peace was upon him,
  and by his wounds we are healed.

We all, like sheep, have gone astray,
  each of us has turned to his own way;
  and the LORD has laid on him
  the iniquity of us all.

He was oppressed and afflicted,
  yet he did not open his mouth;
  he was led like a lamb to the slaughter,
  and as a sheep before her shearers is silent,
  so he did not open his mouth.

By oppression and judgment he was taken away.
  And who can speak of his descendants?
  For he was cut off from the land of the living;
  for the transgression of my people he was stricken.

He was assigned a grave with the wicked,
  and with the rich in his death,
  though he had done no violence,
  nor was any deceit in his mouth.

Reading the account of the trial and crucifixion of Jesus, we see these prophesies being fulfilled. Of particular note is the passage that describes how he remained silent before his accusers. Before the Sanhedrin, Pilate and Herod, Jesus was asked "have you nothing to say?" Note also the passage which describes his death and burial fulfilled in that, although nailed to a cross beside two thieves, he was laid in the tomb of Joseph of Arimathea, a wealthy member of the council of the Sanhedrin.

And finally, in fulfilment of the last line of this prophesy, the only grounds for conviction found against Jesus were that he proclaimed that he was the Messiah. It was impossible for him, even when facing the prospect of unimaginable suffering, to lie or even bend the truth slightly about who he was.

Daniel 9: 25-26
New International Version (NIV)

Know and understand this: From the issuing of the decree to restore and rebuild Jerusalem until the Anointed One, the ruler, comes, there will be seven 'sevens,' and sixty-two 'sevens.' It will be rebuilt with streets and a trench, but in times of trouble. After the sixty-two 'sevens,' the Anointed One will be cut off and will have nothing. The people of the ruler who will come will destroy the city and the sanctuary.

Matthew 24: 1-2
New International Version (NIV)

Jesus left the temple and was walking away when his disciples came up to him to call his attention to its buildings. "Do you see all these things?" he asked. "I tell you the truth, not one stone here will be left on another; every one will be thrown down."

Deuteronomy 28: 49-52
New International Version (NIV)

The LORD will bring a nation against you from far away, from the ends of the earth, like an eagle swooping down, a nation whose language you will not understand, a fierce-looking nation without respect for the old or pity for the young. They will devour the young of your livestock and the crops of your land until you are destroyed. They will leave you no grain, new wine or oil, nor any calves of your herds or lambs of your flocks until you are ruined. They will lay siege to all the cities throughout your land until the high fortified walls in which you trust fall down. They will besiege all the cities throughout the land the LORD your God is giving you.

Here we have three prophesies of the same event or events namely the destruction of Jerusalem, including the temple by the Romans.

The prophesy of Daniel clearly states that the destruction will come following the people's rejection of the "Anointed One" and that it will come at the hand of the people of the ruler.

Rome ruled over Israel for a century before Jewish revolts in 67AD and 132 AD were punished by Roman Armies. The destruction of the temple itself, prophesied by Jesus, occurred in 70AD. Ironic, as the justification for his death sentence was that it would preserve the Jewish nation.

The third prophesy here from Deuteronomy specifies that the army that destroyed Israel would be gathered from the ends of the earth. It is recorded that to quell the Jewish uprising, reinforcements from as far away as the UK were recalled by Rome, whose Standard was commonly that of an eagle.

First century historians noted the ferocity of the destruction of Israel by the Romans which included the destruction of 935 villages.

Deuteronomy 33: 18-19
New International Version (NIV)

About Zebulun he said: "Rejoice, Zebulun, in your going out, and you, Issachar, in your tents.

They will summon peoples to the mountain and there offer sacrifices of righteousness; they will feast on the abundance of the seas, on the treasures hidden in the sand."

To finish, just to show that all prophesies are not related to ancient times, this prophesy wasn't fulfilled until Haifa's Bay became an important port in Mediterranean Sea and the great oil pipeline across Palestine was opened in 1935.

The aforementioned prophesies are merely a quick glimpse into the realm, and hopefully enough to demonstrate that there are rather too many coincidences between biblical prophecy and historical events for us to continue to call them such.

In the UK, which is the only culture I really know intimately, we only really learn our own history, so everything else seems ... well, foreign. To put a British spin on it, some of these prophesies are akin to predicting that Henry VIII would have 6 wives, no legitimate sons, and would be succeeded by his daughter who would turn out to be a stronger ruler than himself.

So what should we take from this? Well hopefully we can benefit from the implicit message that these fulfilments of prophesy represent. In a rebuke to individuals and nations, God speaks in a very person to person manner through Isaiah, proclaiming:

Isaiah 45 19-21
New International Version (NIV)

> *"I have not spoken in secret,*
> *from somewhere in a land of darkness;*
> *I have not said to Jacob's descendants,*
> *'Seek me in vain.'*
> *I, the LORD, speak the truth;*
> *I declare what is right.*

Gather together and come;
assemble, you fugitives from the nations.
Ignorant are those who carry about idols of wood,
who pray to gods that cannot save.

Declare what is to be, present it—
let them take counsel together.
Who foretold this long ago,
who declared it from the distant past?

Was it not I, the LORD ?
And there is no God apart from me,
a righteous God and a Saviour;
there is none but me.

Turn to me and be saved,
all you ends of the earth;
for I am God, and there is no other".

The God of the Bible is referred to as the Alpha and the Omega, the beginning and the end. Through prophesy, the Father of all mankind has demonstrated these qualities, plainly giving us good reason to believe and accept his written word.

A Unique History

A further thing that makes the Bible unique and unparalleled as a historical record of a people is the nature of its content. As a whole, ancient civilizations had no hesitation in recording, proclaiming and making monuments to their victories, as is still the case today, but what other book or monument stands as a testimony of the rebellion and waywardness of a nation and its subsequent humiliating military defeats like the Bible?

John Wesley, the founder of Methodism (1703-1791), with reference to the uniqueness of the manner of the biblical books made this statement:

"This book had to be written by one of three people: good men, bad men or God. It couldn't have been written by good men because they said it was inspired by the revelation of God. Good men don't lie and deceive. It couldn't have been written by bad men because bad men would not write something that would condemn themselves. It leaves only one conclusion. It was given by divine inspiration of God." (John Wesley)

Hopefully I have provided enough evidence to show you that there are good reasons to take the biblical writings seriously. Yet although the Bible could hardly be described as the most recent publication to hit the shelves, how does it still provoke such controversy amongst people? When works of fiction are released that challenge the divinity of Jesus and the authenticity of the Bible, why do they fly off the shelves so? If we are apparently so secular then why do we obsess over such matters?

In answering this I would like to pose another question and ask how much have we changed as people since the time of Jesus? Clearly our world and our societies have become technologically more advanced (Daniel prophesied that in the latter days, knowledge would greatly increase and people would traverse the earth) but do these environmental changes equate to us being fundamentally different creatures than the people of the first century?

When the Disciples questioned Jesus about his return, he provided them with lots of warnings about the events that would begin to appear in the world foreshadowing his coming, followed by this declaration:

Matthew 24:34
New International Version (NIV)

"Truly I tell you, this generation will certainly not pass away until all these things have happened."

Clearly that physical generation did pass away, however, returning to the central theme, the question we ought to ask is: did it pass away *spiritually*? Or is our obsession with hoping to uncover some dark hidden secret about the life of Jesus that makes him less than the son of God merely another Adam searching for a side exit from having to take responsibility for our indiscretions. Certainly the recurring themes of these modern publications and conspiracy theorists have not changed since the heretical Gnostic writings of the second century, to Jewish church interlopers and all the way back to the courts of the Sadducees and Pharisees with Jesus in their midst:

Luke 22:67-74
New International Version (NIV)

"If you are the Messiah," they said, "tell us."

Jesus answered, "If I tell you, you will not believe me, and if I asked you, you would not answer. But from now on, the Son of Man will be seated at the right hand of the mighty God."

They all asked, "Are you then the Son of God?"

He replied, "You say that I am."

Then they said, "Why do we need any more testimony? We have heard it from his own lips."

The central issue is today, as it was yesterday, whether or not Jesus is the Son of God. The Bible is and always will be controversial because of the central figure it talks of and whose words still live and breathe within its pages.

Given a moderate understanding of the teachings of Jesus, with regards to how the man-made systems and man-made wisdoms of the world will receive his message, the continuing furores surrounding him serve only to reinforce the validity of his testimony.

Undeniable evidence

Yet it is neither this, nor the evidential proofs which we briefly touched upon, impressive as they are, that comprise the foundation of our faith in the authenticity of the word.

Faith, in the validity the word, comes primarily for the believer through the person of Holy Spirit. As mystical as this may seem to non-believers, the current incumbent of Jesus' position in the world is the Holy Spirit. It is this presence of the third person of God that means that Jesus did not simply come, show us how it's done and leave us to it.

It is he who quickens the word, confirming its authorship, as the Bible speaks into our daily lives and situations, resonating in our hearts thousands of years after it was written that is a far greater testimony and source of confidence in its authorship than any study.

Like the book in the 80's film the Neverending Story, where a bookworm boy called Sebastian receives a mysterious book unlike anything he has ever read before, this Bible is not 'safe' like other books. As Sebastian reads his book about a quest to save a magical land, he finds as it progresses that the book is speaking to him and about him and that he has become part of the story to the point where the characters begin to call his name.

The truth, in this instance, is stranger than fiction; as the Holy Spirit opens up the words of the Bible to our hearts we can become aware that this is no ordinary book and that we are the reason for its existence and that it is for us that its central figure came and gave his life.

We read in Luke how, following the crucifixion and even after the reports of the resurrection by Mary and Martha, two Disciples were nevertheless returning to their former lives. On the road they are joined by Jesus, posing as a stranger, who in discussion opens up scriptures to them so that their "hearts burned within them". This is the work of the Holy Spirit. If the Bible is not burning in our hearts then we ought to seek God in prayer for the Holy Spirit to do just that for us.

In conclusion, if these are, after all, the words of God to humanity, is there not a measure of hope in the fact that rarely do people easily grasp the depth of meaning found within its pages. For as I believe I have already stated, but it's worth stating again, that if there is any hope to be found in God then it is that he is not like Man and that Man, though of God and with a capacity to serve as God's representative, has in fact drifted far from his source and has need to return?

May God add his blessing to what you have read and may you dwell forever in the light of his presence.

The Bible and Sex

If I was to be completely honest, and despite the mental gymnastics of eastern philosophy trying to work a way around it, sex had been a part of life that even as an adult I hadn't completely come to terms with. The question: "Should we be doing it or shouldn't we?" had never been completely put to bed – if you'll pardon the pun. Maintaining the idea that the continued disturbances of my conscience were the side effects of a Christianized society, subliminally sowing some bad seed in my pre-adolescence, became impossible as I had ploughed my consciousness thoroughly long ago through self observation and meditation and had neither regarded, nor paid heed to, anything remotely biblical on this subject since. The undeniable testimony of which was the two children I now had.

Yet accidental fatherhood, invading my well laid out plans as it did, had found me ill prepared for the cold stone floor seriousness of adult responsibilities and brought situations that required a man of greater integrity than myself. Ultimately it would be the need for authoritative answers, for questions about my responsibilities to my young family that would bring me to church the Sunday I received Jesus.

As I began anew, I had to accept in retrospect that whatever the best way to handle physical relationships was, one thing was certain, the path I had mapped for myself to date was not it. What would I find the Bible saying about sex and relationships though? (To be honest, living with the mother of my two children, I wasn't in any desperate rush to start noting down scripture references.) Was the Bible going to confirm the Catholic stereotype of condemning all things sex related? Was I expected to hate Gay people now as a Christian? Or perhaps the Bible would set standards that were just impossible to live to in these times.

In what follows I will share my findings to date, but that is not to say that I haven't still much to learn. Whilst my goal, as previously, will be to allay as many commonly held ill gotten misconceptions as possible, I promise also that I will try to be as sensitive as possible to those for whom this has been a source of distress.

To begin with, I believe that the central issue that leads to understanding all questions related to sex is one we have already uncovered. This question being:

What are we ultimately?

Are we flesh? Destined for the grave, and the worms and woodlice?

Or are we spirit? Bound to an eternal destiny and an appointment with our maker?

It is important we clarify where we stand on this. If we are flesh then our sexual desires are simply part of the whole of that which we are and we have every reason to banish all doubt on the subject. Or if we are in truth spirit and of heavenly origin, then we ought rightly to ask why we find these desires can persistently occupy such a prominent place in our thinking?

The answer I proposed earlier, and the understanding we gain from the Bible, on this conundrum with which we are confronted daily is that we are in fact both. In that we exist as an eternal spirit dwelling within a temporary mortal frame.

We would do well to make it an imperative, before we approach this issue, to understand this and appropriate the understanding to our own situation, because it is by ways of this dual nature that we find conflicting forces at work within us, before we even get started with addressing the idea of a spiritual enemy also at work putting his two-penneth into the mix.

A double nature means a double agenda. One, the soul or spirit, has an eternal perspective and seeks to ensure its own well-being (such as preparing for a life without the body). Whilst the other has a shorter life expectancy and seeks to get what it can, while it can. The crux of the matter then is this: that making the fulfilment of the body's desires our priority, whether that is for food, sex, drink or whatever will always involve the spiritual longings of our soul taking a back seat. This is simply the nature of conflict. Sooner or later in life one or the other has to take precedence, in other words: one or the other will generally hold sway in our lives.

Now in this conflict there is a catch to do with our spiritual inheritance which tips the odds of our soul coming out on top against us.

You may by now be unsurprised to find that we will again return to the Garden of Eden narrative for answers. Whether you are willing or not to accept the narrative as a physical truth, spiritually there is much to gain in relation to this conflict from its assessment of our situation: the infamous narrative's message, that inherent within the nature of mankind is a weakness to place the desire to fulfil the longings of our mortal frame over and above our spiritual calling, is clear.

I am not about to contradict myself and start saying that the whole of Adam and Eve thing is all about them having it off now, just to clarify; the fleshy desire in the Garden was, if you recall, for food. Sex actually makes its appearance way before the famed scenario gets going, whilst Adam and Eve are still on the right track, God blesses them with the task of populating the world!

To clarify a further misconception: by talking about spiritually inherited weaknesses we aren't perpetuating the idea that newborn babies are riddled with sins either. There is what the Bible talks of, even with regards to Jesus, an age of responsibility when a person is able to differentiate between right and wrong and therefore becomes responsible for their actions.

Neither does the Bible say that there is anything implicitly wrong with satisfying physical desires when they hold the correct position in our lives. Adam and Eve's problem was eating; obviously we have to eat, but the problem arises when seeking these God-given pleasures takes priority over fulfilling our purposes in God.

Matthew 22: 36-40
New International Version (NIV)

"Teacher, which is the greatest commandment in the Law?"

Jesus replied: "'Love the Lord your God with all your heart and with all your soul and with all your mind.' This is the first and greatest commandment. And the second is like it: 'Love your neighbour as yourself.' All the Law and the Prophets hang on these two commandments."

The commandment above, "Love the Lord your God with all your heart and with all your soul and with all your mind" cannot be fulfilled if our priority is getting all the short-term pleasure we can. That command is "Love physical pleasure with all your heart and with all your soul and with all your mind".

Should we still have doubts about our current inclination, or even that such conflicts exist, then it might be worth reminding ourselves that the world of advertising and popular culture has sussed our weaknesses long ago, utilising the promise of the fulfilment of our fleshy longings to lend allure to just about anything.

So where does this leave us?

There is a change in the very heart of Man that needs to happen before we can live victoriously and peacefully with the conflicting desires of our soul and flesh warring within us, of which our desire for sex is one. Paul describes the Law of Moses as a school master that makes our inability to live right before God painfully obvious. The recorded history of the nation of Israel is in part a testimony to this fact. Put simply: for God to just to say "don't do this and that or the other" and "do this and this", isn't enough for us. What that actually does is make our inability to live by God's standards more apparent, serving only to highlight the need for a revolution within.

This revolution in the attitude of our hearts toward God is a change that we cannot make ourselves any more than the Queen could bring about an anti-monarchist uprising against herself. We are the pot in Jeremiah and the pot cannot reshape itself; we need to return to the potter to make us anew.

Jeremiah 18: 1-6
New International Version (NIV)

This is the word that came to Jeremiah from the Lord: "Go down to the potter's house, and there I will give you my message." So I went down to the potter's house, and I saw him working at the wheel. But the pot he was shaping from the clay was marred in his hands; so the potter formed it into another pot, shaping it as seemed best to him.

Then the word of the Lord came to me. He said, "Can I not do with you, Israel, as this potter does?" declares the Lord. "Like clay in the hand of the potter, so are you in my hand, Israel".

It is through Jesus that we are able to approach God and invite him to enact this change in our hearts that includes, amongst many other blessings, the tipping of the balance of power in this conflict in favour of our spirit. No longer are we inclined toward pursuing our fleshy desires over and above our purposes in God. It is simply no longer possible for our lives to be directed by the fruitless and redundant longings of the flesh, once we encounter and continue to spend time in the presence of Him who is the fulfilment of the very deepest longings of our soul as He leads and comforts us through life.

Psalm 16: 11
New King James Version (NKJV)

You will show me the path of life;
In Your presence is fullness of joy;
At Your right hand are pleasures forevermore.

Hosea 4: 6, speaking of the decline of Israel, declares that *"the children perish for lack of knowledge"* and if there is one discernible shift in popular culture that I have noticed in my lifetime, that seems most damaging, it would have to be the popular acceptance of living a compromised or a disempowered adult life with regards to this conflict in all its various forms.

Without knowing the empowering joy of salvation, or anything about repentance, the default position we assume, in face of a rudimentary half-knowledge of the legalistic requirements of religion, is one of compromise, as outside of God our hearts are not naturally inclined towards repentance or seeking God out to fix our problems. "If at first you don't succeed, lower your standards" has become our comical motto and as long as we are all living it, and laughing about ourselves whilst living it, who is going to tell us that there is anything else? Perhaps understandably, seeing as they don't recognise Jesus yet, the popular TV sit-coms of Jewish origin are often of this ilk.

Yet we don't have to be compromised. We can live at peace with our conflicting desires once we allow the Holy Spirit to bring about order within us. We can change in God and become the people God created us to be, men and women of our Father embodying His power and love. Temptations will still come, yes, and maybe at times we will fail, but any misadventures we may have, as long we remain in Jesus, will be against the flow of our lives as we move from victory to victory trusting in our saviour and king.

What the Bible says specifically about sex

In a marriage between a man and a woman, the Bible is clear that sex carries no baggage with it. Among the heroes of the Bible its central figure is the exception to the rule, most of the supporting cast have active sex lives with no negative associations attributed.

However there is a further question implicit in this: How does the Bible define marriage?

Surprisingly, the Bible doesn't actually contain any formal rules or dictates about marriage ceremony. In the Garden we here that Adam and Eve become one flesh through "knowing each other" or in other words making love and are therefore life partners.

We first hear of a ceremony of marriage in the Law of Moses which made it clear that a woman ought not to have had sex before she was married and that in the case of a woman being seduced by a man before marriage, as long as her father didn't object, they ought to become Man and Wife from that point on.

I am not trying to scare anyone here. I am just pointing out that, in biblical terms, sex and marriage are intertwined. Even today in English law a marriage is not considered complete until the couple have jumped in the marriage sack together; until then it can still be annulled, after that point any break up is regarded as divorce.

Matthew 19: 3-8
New International Version (NIV)

Some Pharisees came to him to test him. They asked, "Is it lawful for a man to divorce his wife for any and every reason?"

"Haven't you read," he replied, "that at the beginning the Creator 'made them male and female,' and said, 'For this reason a man will leave his father and mother and be united to his wife, and the two will become one flesh'? So they are no longer two, but one flesh. Therefore what God has joined together, let no one separate."

"Why then," they asked, "did Moses command that a man give his wife a certificate of divorce and send her away?"

Jesus replied, "Moses permitted you to divorce your wives because your hearts were hard. But it was not this way from the beginning".

Although divorce was legalised through the Law of Moses we gain from Jesus the understanding that this was a temporary concession to avoid mistreatment of women and not what was intended for mankind.

There may be no formal dictates for marriage ceremonies in the Bible but there are undeniable proofs that the practice meets the approval of God: Jesus referred to his return and physical reunion with his church as a marriage and performed his first miracle, of turning water into wine for the guests at a wedding reception, to name two examples. However, the fact that such a ceremony has not occurred does not mean that two people are not joined in the eyes of God. Returning to the statement of Jesus, with regards to divorce, Jesus clearly considered Adam and Eve to be Man and wife.

Clearly I have not lived this, so judgement does not form any part of my purpose in this, but having seen the other options through the separation of my parents and only the grace of God sparing my children from their own 21st century re-run of it all, I would suggest that there are practical merits to keeping sex within the confines of marriage. Contraception is not all it's cracked up to be for one and adhering to these principals can save generations of heartache for adults and children alike.

From an emotional perspective also, sex is the most physically intimate thing that two people can do together and although we may be full of bravado at times, only the individual and God truly know what is going on in the heart of a person, so how do we know what emotional effect our actions are having? Should we become so familiar with sex that it becomes devoid of any sense of intimacy

OH NO NOT JESUS

THE BIBLE AND SEX

or emotional meaning, aren't we then drastically devaluing the whole thing to our own hurt?

For those who see this as unliveable I would heartily agree. Because outside of Jesus in our modern world it is highly unlikely that we would not have sex before we are married. That's why Jesus says:

Matthew 6: 33
New International Version (NIV)

But seek first his kingdom and his righteousness, and all these things will be given to you as well.

This is contrary to our culture which tells us to seek first sex, a car, a house, foreign holidays a big wedding.

I know I'm repeating myself, but I'm not casting judgement on anyone but in humility, myself, looking back now I think doing it Jesus' way would have been a more honourable way for me to behave and what my wife truly deserves.

Homosexuality

To end on a light hearted note (this is written sarcasm here). If God is concerned first and foremost with the attitude of our hearts toward Him, our spirit or soul, then why does it matter what gender the person we choose to have a relationship with is?

Firstly this argument implies that spiritually we are asexual which is unbiblical. Separate definable spiritual qualities are attributed by gender in the biblical scheme of things:

Genesis 2: 21-22
New International Version (NIV)

So the Lord God caused the man to fall into a deep sleep; and while he was sleeping, he took one of the man's ribs and then closed up the place with flesh. Then the Lord God made a woman

*from the rib he had taken out of the man, and he brought her to
the man.*

By ways of the depiction of God extracting woman from man (if we
find this is offensive then hang fire – we will get on to
understanding the precise tone of the original text of this in the
chapter "Women and the Bible" which offers some surprises) we
gain the understanding that part of what originally made humanity
was taken away permanently from man to make his companion.
Prior to this then we must assume that man embodied within him
all the characteristics of human nature.

Since the creation of woman, if man was ever to have all the
qualities gifted to the human race by God, he was going to have to
be joined to woman. Hence the line in the preceding quote from
Matthew about "For this reason a man will leave his father and
mother…" which is taken from Genesis. In the biblical scheme of
things humanity is a whole in two parts. Given enough life
experience most people will happily accept that men and women
generally possess a differing set of identifiable generic qualities.
Biblically it is the balance of these qualities in the context of
marriage that provides the foundation of all the blessings of God to
humanity in one place, making it also the perfect environment for
bringing up children.

If spiritual wholeness in relationships is God's plan and this can only
be achieved when a man and woman are joined, same sex
relationships become spiritually redundant as they do not fall in line
with God's purposes. If it is spiritually redundant then the physical,
sexual side of it all is prioritising desire over and above our purpose
in God, which constitutes a rejection of God and His purposes.

(It might be a timely point to remind ourselves that we are speaking
under the assumed acceptance of the possibility of getting answers
direct from God on the biggest questions. If we can know that the
God of the Bible is truly who it says He is and that the Bible is His
word, then we can be assured that He is not going to set someone

on a course that contradicts what's in it. When it comes to His word it is not a case of different strokes for different folks.)

If we are passionately determined to refute this, then we need to place our hands on our heart and say that a man can be as truly womanly as a woman and alternately that a woman can be as manly as a man, for that matter.

Personally, having worked with and consider as friends people who would describe themselves as homosexual, I have still never been convinced. Do I believe for example, that a man could exude the loving tenderness that I saw in my wife when she held our children for the first time after they were born? Or possess the intuitive awareness of our child's needs in those first few weeks?

Let us not be so overly intellectual and pompous to just say it as it is. No.

1 Corinthians 6: 9-11
New International Version (NIV)

Or do you not know that wrongdoers will not inherit the kingdom of God? Do not be deceived: Neither the sexually immoral nor idolaters nor adulterers nor men who have sex with men nor thieves nor the greedy nor drunkards nor slanderers nor swindlers will inherit the kingdom of God. And that is what some of you were. But you were washed, you were sanctified, you were justified in the name of the Lord Jesus Christ and by the Spirit of our God.

The Christian community is not at war with the homosexual community, but it is at war with the enemy of our souls who deceives and entices mankind into rebellion against his creator within his heart, which is then expressed through his actions. The form of expression that this inner rebellion takes is not the issue.

The issue is our hearts and their alignment to God and his purposes.

The media often lends a voice to Church of England members who advocate the acceptance of homosexuality in the Church on the basis of there being no identifiable role model in scripture for a loving relationship of this kind. But in reality, the idea that relationships of this kind didn't exist in ancient times is far-fetched. It is well known that homosexuality was accepted and common place in Roman culture as it was in Grecian culture and just about every other culture you care to identify. The uncomfortable truth is that, in light of these, the Bible is unequivocal that such a lifestyle is at odds with the standards of holiness that God created his earthly representatives for. The Bible is equally unequivocal that such a lifestyle does not exclude a person from being a candidate for salvation or the love of Jesus Christ.

So Someone 2000 Years Ago Died on a Cross... And?

Whether or not we understand the message of the Cross, we can nevertheless experience its accomplishment. Stood at the Altar of Leeds New Testament Church of God, repeating the prayer that the Pastor dictated to me, I hadn't really attempted to understand what the Cross signified in any depth. All I knew was that there was more to this Jesus stuff than I had previously thought and that if I was going to move forward, from the crossroads in life that I found myself at with a clear conscience, then I had to be sure that I had made myself available to hear from God directly.

Thankfully in what followed I am not alone, countless testimonies from all walks of life today, as they always have, concur with my own story that, two thousand years after His death outside of the walls of Jerusalem, calling on God in Jesus' name changes everything. Chains of addiction, chains of emotional and physical abuse and snares of our own making, of any variety you might care to name, are all loosed in an instant, their former potency extinguished, as a new presence that begins to work in our hearts following our acknowledgement of the Cross as our own personal redemptive plan.

The question we want to address here though is 'How?'

How can the death of Jesus have any possible impact on a person's life today, tomorrow or yesterday?

What is meant to have occurred on the Cross that brought about the availability of such transforming power?

As you may by now have become accustomed, there is a limit to what I will be able to cram into this brief overview, so attempting to communicate every facet of the Cross is out. That thousands of hymns and books and sermons have done a far greater service to this subject than I will in these few pages is something I accept from the outset. My limited aim then will be to present an introduction to the prequel to the Cross that exists in the repeated pattern of its types throughout the Bible, prior to the life and ministry of Jesus. This understanding, as a context for the Cross, will hopefully take us deeper into its message and support the eternal/spiritual boasts of the Cross' accomplishment that is also the core of Jesus' teaching: that he and he alone is the saviour of all mankind both now and forevermore.

Firstly, there is of course a very straightforward and simple message that the Cross has been effectively communicating for centuries:

That God loves us.

John 3:16
New International Version (NIV)

For God so loved the world that he gave his one and only Son, that whoever believes in him shall not perish but have eternal life.

Like most aspects of the life of Jesus, unsurprisingly there are those who would cast aspersions against this simple timeless message, so let us remind ourselves of the basic facts of the Cross before we go any further:

1: Jesus was afraid of the Cross.

Matthew 26: 36-38
New International Version (NIV)

Then Jesus went with his disciples to a place called Gethsemane, and he said to them, "Sit here while I go over there and pray." He took Peter and the two sons of Zebedee along with him, and he began to be sorrowful and troubled. Then he said to them, "My soul is overwhelmed with sorrow to the point of death. Stay here and keep watch with me."

From simply a physical point of view, the flogging ordered by Pontius Pilate, as means of placating the Jewish leaders, was in itself often enough to kill a man and exceeded the maximum number of lashes that would be administered under the Jewish penal code of the time.

2: Jesus had the power available to him to prevent the crucifixion at any given time.

Matthew 26: 52-54
New International Version (NIV)

"Put your sword back in its place," Jesus said to him, "for all who draw the sword will die by the sword. Do you think I cannot call on my Father, and he will at once put at my disposal more than twelve legions of angels? But how then would the Scriptures be fulfilled that say it must happen in this way?"

3: Yet as referenced in the previous scripture he endured the Cross because he understood that it was the will of God for his life

Matthew 26: 39
New International Version (NIV)

Going a little farther, he fell with his face to the ground and prayed, "My Father, if it is possible, may this cup be taken from me. Yet not as I will, but as you will."

4: Jesus was sent to the Cross for one reason and one reason only, that he proclaimed that he was the Son of God and the promised Messiah, spoken of through the prophets, in the Old Testament.

Matthew 26: 63-68
New King James Version (NKJV)

But Jesus kept silent. And the high priest answered and said to Him, "I put you under oath by the living God: Tell us if you are the Christ, the Son of God!"

Jesus said to him, "It is as you said. Nevertheless, I say to you, hereafter you will see the Son of Man sitting at the right hand of the Power, and coming on the clouds of heaven."

Then the high priest tore his clothes, saying, "He has spoken blasphemy! What further need do we have of witnesses? Look, now you have heard His blasphemy! What do you think?"

They answered and said, "He is deserving of death."

Then they spat in His face and beat Him; and others struck Him with the palms of their hands, saying, "Prophesy to us, Christ! Who is the one who struck you?"

Faced with the choice of life if he denies who he is and of death if he doesn't, Jesus confirms his own death sentence with a triumphant prophetic message of his eternal victory.

5. That Jesus died on the Cross

John 19:34
New International Version (NIV)

Instead, one of the soldiers pierced Jesus' side with a spear, bringing a sudden flow of blood and water.

Modern day knowledge of the human body helps us to understand that more than likely the excruciating agony of crucifixion would send the victim into hypovolemic shock or alternatively, due to the expansion of the chest muscles from the victim supporting themselves by their outstretched arms, death could be caused by asphyxiation, the consequences of which include water collecting in the sack surrounding the heart or water collecting on the lungs. The spear thrust in to his side was no hesitant pin prick but was meant as a decisive strike, the appearance of water prior to a flow of blood deeming the common practise of breaking a victim's legs to quicken their death unnecessary.

(Due to this testimony pre-dating the medical knowledge, this extract from the gospel of John adds further credence to this being an eyewitness account)

Circumstantial evidence like this is what is often overlooked by those seeking to dispute the scriptural accounts. For example, in the case of the argument of whether Jesus openly proclaimed he was the Son of God? Yes he did, but not only that, to those who knew the Old Testament scriptures he was, by his actions, continually and deliberately proclaiming himself as such. Furthermore with regards to the theory that Jesus didn't really die on the Cross, then why lay him in a tomb and return there on that first Easter Sunday, with spices to prepare his body for burial as the women did? Why did the disciples, bereaved and perplexed, begin then to return to their former lives?

Realistically, such questions fall under the umbrella of the questioning the character of Jesus, suggesting that Jesus was somehow part of some grand deception that is again at odds with the life and character of the servant leader, healer and defender of the poor.

Moving on...

Luke 24: 25-27
New International Version (NIV)

He said to them, "How foolish you are, and how slow to believe all that the prophets have spoken! Did not the Messiah have to suffer these things and then enter his glory?"And beginning with Moses and all the Prophets, he explained to them what was said in all the Scriptures concerning himself.

Clearly from this scripture we see that the Cross, as far as Jesus was concerned, was not without precedent and something the Disciples who were all heading their separate ways, here, after their teacher of the past three years had been apparently killed, ought to have understood from the Old Testament scriptures.

Jesus in the Old Testament

From a broad perspective, after reading the main stories in the Bible and hearing a few sermons we become aware that the lives of the biblical heroes all reflect Jesus' life in ways which cannot be merely coincidental. For an outline of the subject:

Moses in the book of Exodus was born at a time when young male babies were being exterminated, as Jesus was. He grew up as royalty in Pharaoh's palace but gave up his position as royalty to be considered as an ordinary Hebrew because of his compassion for his suffering people. For his trouble he was rejected by his kindred *(Jesus was rejected by his own people the Israelites)*. Nevertheless he returned, was validated before his people as a servant of God by miraculous signs and led them to freedom after 400 years of slavery to the most powerful force upon the earth by his wholehearted trust, dependence and obedience to God. Moses was renowned for the intimate manner of his communication with God.

Yet it is not Moses, the law giver, but Joshua (Jesus is the Greek version of Joshua which means "The Lord Saves") as captain of the Army who leads a second and more faithful generation of God's people across the Jordan. Yet it is not the "rod of correction" that Moses used *(symbolic of the written law)* to part the waters of the Red Sea but it is the current physical representation of the presence of God (the Ark of the Covenant) that holds within it the words, written by God himself *(the Ten Commandments here but Jesus declared that he only spoke words given to him by his father)*, that halts the flow of the river Jordan from the city of "Adam" to the Dead Sea! Therefore, symbolically, here God provides an otherwise impossible passage across the overflowing, consuming tide that would carry every man to his death, by standing in the gap himself between Adam and death until all his people pass safely across into the promises of God. *(The river Jordan flows into the Dead Sea the lowest point on the globe, not that anyone could have known that at the time. Hence the symbolic nature of being baptised in the river Jordan and the rebellion or sin of your former life being dead and buried).*

At the conclusion of Genesis we have the life of Jesus typified in Joseph. The beloved son of his father rejected and betrayed by his own brothers, out of jealousy for their father's affections toward him, into slavery in Egypt *(symbolic of slavery and captivity throughout the Bible).* Yet through his unswerving commitment and trust in the providence of God, through all his trials, he is exalted to the highest position of power in the land to reign over the nation that was once his jailer. From here he becomes the forgiving saviour of his now repentant brothers, from starvation and ruin, who are the very founders of the twelve tribes of Israel.

Despite being anointed by the Prophet Samuel at a young age to be the future King of Israel, David again was maligned initially by his brothers. Sent to the battlefront by his father to bring back a report on how his father's children were getting along, David is accused at the battle by his eldest brother of having a "wicked heart". Goliath taunts the Armies of Israel for 40 days and 40 nights yet, in an unexpected fashion and through his complete trust in God, David defeats Goliath all by himself, winning a battle for all the people that, if he had lost, would have made the Israelites slaves to the Philistines forever. In addition to this, although God had pronounced judgement upon the current ruler and announced David as King, Saul continues to reign for a time. While David is in exile, the indebted, the discontented and the desperate seek him out to join with him and have him as their captain. Eventually David returns as King over all Israel as originally prophesied by Samuel, foreshadowing the promise of the second coming of Jesus Christ.

Going even further back into Genesis, the life of Christ is typified way before Joseph in Isaac, the long awaited, divinely promised only son of Abraham and Sarah through whom it was promised would come descendants that would be more numerous than the stars in the sky *(remember there's no street lights back then!)*, who carries the sticks for his own sacrifice up the very the same mountain where Christ would eventually be crucified! Who also, on questioning his father Abraham on the whereabouts of the obligatory animal for the proposed sacrifice, receives the cryptic answer: "The Lord will provide for himself a lamb"!

Now it is not that God wants to tell scary stories to children, God doesn't and never has demanded human sacrifice, hence why Abraham is prevented from killing his son! Yet the despicable horror, which Abraham and we are spared from experiencing, God did not spare himself when his sent his own son in to the world to die on a Cross! If the thought of sacrificing a teenager is horrific then how horrific is the willing sacrifice of Jesus at the hands of those he came to save? The whole point God is making here and the reason such extreme cultural boundary crossing metaphors are employed, such as the senseless death of an only son, is so that the great depth of love that he has for mankind can be communicated as fully as it is possible for the human heart to comprehend.

Kept from harming his son, both Isaac and Abraham rejoice as they turn and see the previously unnoticed Ram with its horns caught in a thicket that would take Isaac's place as the sacrifice. Abraham, doubtless relieved, calls to the place, "The Lord will provide", and coins a phrase: "On the mount of the Lord it will be provided" pointing forward to Jesus, "The Lamb of God", who would carry his cross up the same Calvary, his head crowned in his own thicket of thorns in our place.

The Substitute

A key principle in understanding the pattern God uses, and that the Cross in particular adheres to, is the Old Testament principle of a substitute sacrifice for the atonement of Man's rebellion. To our ears, this seems like an abhorrent practise from the dark recesses of time but understood in its context the principle is not as reprehensible as it first seems.

Israel, the chosen people, so cherished and upheld by God like no other people before them, were, for a generation after leaving Egypt, a travelling people whose only wealth was their herds. Offering the best of their most valuable possession, rather than being some pagan orgy of blood, was in truth a costly act of self-sacrifice made in acknowledgement of a personal debt owed to God by the individual. The aim of which was to seek the reconciliation and restoration of their relationship to God, their having broken the Law of Moses bearing witness to their rejection and separation from him. The offer, acknowledging the just reward for their opposition to God, made now in strict accordance with his will was a symbolic gesture of their willingness above all else to return to be part of their Father's purposes and a petition to the inherent goodness and mercy of God.

The forgiveness that they received through the acceptance of the substitute offering was not something that the act of offering purchased the individual as a necessity but, offered in the right spirit, with a repentant heart, the unmerited favour (grace) of God was bestowed upon the giver and their transgression of the law forgiven as their gift, by virtue of its echoing the eventual fulfilment of its type in the crucifixion of Jesus Christ, moves the heart of God.

Going deeper there is more this principle has to tell us about the work of the Cross.

The Blood

Leviticus 17: 11
King James Version (KJV)

For the life of the flesh is in the blood: and I have given it to you upon the altar to make an atonement for your souls: for it is the blood that maketh an atonement for the soul.

Exodus 24: 6-8
New International Version (NIV)

Moses took half of the blood and put it in bowls, and the other half he splashed against the altar. Then he took the Book of the Covenant and read it to the people. They responded, "We will do everything the Lord has said; we will obey."

Moses then took the blood, sprinkled it on the people and said, "This is the blood of the covenant that the Lord has made with you in accordance with all these words."

The blood of this self-sacrificial offering, in terms of the Old Testament, had three specific symbolic purposes: It was shed for the forgiveness of sins, daubed or sprinkled for the sealing of a covenant and sprinkled for purification.

Before anyone goes and kills their pet on the top of the nearest hill and starts flicking its blood on folks, let's remind ourselves that what was instituted in these practises was a physical pattern of the eternal spiritual reality finally unveiled in the Cross, the centrepiece of the New Covenant.

So our pets are safe.

Every section of the travelling community of shepherds would be able to easily relate to the solemnity of the experience of the death of an innocent lamb and easily be able to appropriate the "blood equals life" principle from the preceding scripture, when witnessing the light in the eyes of the animal dim as its blood leaves its body.

Spiritually, what these types communicate to us is that the presence of God within our lives is akin to the blood of our souls. It is the spirit of God within us that is our fountain of joy, that ought to be flowing through us always giving vitality to our hearts, that is our true life that extends beyond the limits of our physical frame, without which we inevitably die.

Our rejection of God that results in separation from his presence initiates the spiritual equivalent of our physical blood draining out of our bodies. As the blood of animals was to be understood as belonging not to Man but to God, so our souls are to be devoted to God and not Man.

The High Priest

In addition to individual sacrifices offered for specific transgressions of the law as part of the Old Covenant or agreement, there were also ordinances for general offerings for all the people, which has obvious parallels in the Cross. Once a year, after rigorous ritualistic cleansing, a High Priest would be selected to go beyond the veil of the temple into the Holy of Holies, where traditionally the Ark of the Covenant (the physical representation of God's presence) was kept, to offer a sacrifice for the sin of the whole nation. Known as Yom Kippur, or The Day of Atonement (note: At-one-ment), God would appear to the High Priest in a cloud over the lid of the Ark and confirm that their petition for mercy had been granted.

Where the Israelites fell into error is when they perverted the meaning of these ordinances so that their self-sacrificial offerings became a way of scoring them points in heaven. From there, inward rebellion to God became unimportant, as long as you were scoring enough points with God in the tabernacle or temple to balance it all out. This is evidenced in the Old Testament where, once God had prospered his people and settled them in their own land, out of their wealth they began to offer ostentatious sacrifices which Isaiah records became an offence to God.

Isaiah 1: 11-17
New International Version (NIV)

"The multitude of your sacrifices what are they to me?" says the LORD. I have more than enough of burnt offerings, of rams and the fat of fattened animals; I have no pleasure in the blood of bulls and lambs and goats.

When you come to appear before me, who has asked this of you, this trampling of my courts? Stop bringing meaningless offerings! Your incense is detestable to me. New Moons, Sabbaths and convocations I cannot bear your worthless assemblies.

Your New Moon feasts and your appointed festivals I hate with all my being. They have become a burden to me I am weary of bearing them. When you spread out your hands in prayer, I hide my eyes from you; even when you offer many prayers, I am not listening.

Your hands are full of blood!

Wash and make yourselves clean. Take your evil deeds out of my sight; stop doing wrong. Learn to do right; seek justice. Defend the oppressed. Take up the cause of the fatherless; plead the case of the widow".

God desires "truth in the inmost parts", wrote David, yet the Israelites' hearts became hard and the commands they received from God were treated as merely external ordinances. Yet God promises to change the situation.

Ezekiel 36: 26-27
New International Version (NIV)

"I will give you a new heart and put a new spirit in you; I will remove from you your heart of stone and give you a heart of flesh. And I will put my Spirit in you and move you to follow my decrees and be careful to keep my laws."

The inability of mankind to be true to God within the bounds of the law highlighted that, collectively, the work wrought at Man's inception still held sway within his heart. Also it served, as stated in previous chapters, to highlight that rebellion was not merely an action but an indwelling disposition of the heart. This was why the teachings of Jesus went further than that of Moses. For example, in his sermon on the mount, Jesus takes the laws of Moses and directs his followers away from the external action and to the source of the problem:

Matthew 5: 27-28
New International Version (NIV)

"You have heard that it was said, 'You shall not commit adultery.' But I tell you that anyone who looks at a woman lustfully has already committed adultery with her in his heart."

Similarly, by virtue of their obedience to the letter of the law, the religious elite of Jesus' time considered themselves "clean". Yet Jesus saw it rather differently.

Matthew 23: 25-26
New International Version (NIV)

"Woe to you, teachers of the law and Pharisees, you hypocrites! You clean the outside of the cup and dish, but inside they are full of greed and self-indulgence. Blind Pharisee! First clean the inside of the cup and dish, and then the outside also will be clean."

Jesus explained this transition of focus as not an abolishment of the Law of Moses but the fulfilment of it. To take the pattern of it in other words, and make it effective upon the heart. We see this in the Cross where the pattern of the self-sacrificial offering is repeated physically, albeit in a far more reprehensible scenario, in that the physical blood of Jesus is shed, yet the focus and aim was clearly spiritual:

Luke 23:46
New International Version (NIV)

Jesus called out with a loud voice, "Father, into your hands I commit my spirit." When he had said this, he breathed his last.

By virtue of Jesus having led a life free from rebellion to God, adhering to the pattern of the Law's requirement for a lamb without blemish, Jesus died with his relationship to God still intact, the first and last experience of separation from the Father coming when he took upon himself the just reward of Man's rebellion:

Offering himself physically at Calvary, he was also presenting himself as an offering before God on the heavenly spiritual Altar, as the heavenly High Priest of Yom Kippur, for the sin of all mankind. The eternal blood of his soul/spirit poured out before God is the seal of the new covenant in which his unwarranted death becomes the atoning, eternal and therefore eternally applicable self-sacrifice for our forgiveness and the cleansing of our hearts. Thus the presence of God becomes available for all in his name.

No need for the veil anymore then:

Matthew 27: 50-51
New International Version (NIV)

And when Jesus had cried out again in a loud voice, he gave up his spirit.

At that moment the curtain of the temple was torn in two from top to bottom. The earth shook, the rocks split

The important difference between this offering and the offerings of the Old Covenant/Agreement and the reason gifts are exchanged at Christmas, being that the offering here is from God whilst the debt owed is Man's.

Our own personal experience of this accomplishment that comes by acknowledging Jesus as the gift of God to humanity, for the payment of our own debt owed to God, is the overwhelming outworking of an emphatic victory of God over the Devil.

As the sword of Joshua the warrior cuts deeper than the rod of Moses, in the new agreement founded in Jesus' death, the deception sown in the very heart of Man at his inception is dealt with in the Cross.

The Anti-Adam

This work is emphasized further by the pattern of Jesus' reversal of the failings of Adam that can be clearly observed in his life:

Whereas Adam, placed in paradise, became mistrustful of God and sought to become as God himself, Jesus, though he was God in heaven, humbled himself to become a man and sought only to serve as a man.

Where Adam, tempted by the devil, headed his voice and adhered to his teaching, Jesus quoted scripture, clinging to God's teaching.

Where Adam through his single act of rebellion at the beginning of time caused the falling into error, resulting in death, of all that would follow him, Jesus, through obedience to death on the Cross, pays the price for everyone to the end of time, bringing eternal life to all that would follow him.

With the separation of our rebellion removed, once again we are able to walk and talk with God His spirit as the blood of our souls renewing, cleansing and reviving our once cold hearts. The only sacrifice required of us being that we stop pretending to be capable and happy being our own Gods.

The Passover Lamb

John 6: 53
New International Version (NIV)

Jesus said to them, "Very truly I tell you, unless you eat the flesh of the Son of Man and drink his blood, you have no life in you."

As the Israelites remembered how they were freed from Pharaoh, Jesus fulfilled the type of the Passover lamb in the spiritual Passover for all humanity. The cleansing work of the Holy Spirit, the presence of God that dwells within those who had been reconciled to God through him, being the spiritual parallel of the lifeblood of the Passover lamb daubed on the doorposts and lintels of the dwellings of the Israelites, applied with Hyssop (symbolic of cleansing).

As the remembrance of the first Passover was an ordinance for the Jewish nation so this second Passover was instituted as an ordinance to be observed by the followers of Jesus.

Luke 22: 15-20
New International Version (NIV)

And he said to them, "I have eagerly desired to eat this Passover with you before I suffer. For I tell you, I will not eat it again until it finds fulfilment in the kingdom of God."

After taking the cup, he gave thanks and said, "Take this and divide it among you. For I tell you I will not drink again from the fruit of the vine until the kingdom of God comes."

And he took bread, gave thanks and broke it, and gave it to them, saying, "This is my body given for you; do this in remembrance of me."

In the same way, after the supper he took the cup, saying, "This cup is the new covenant in my blood, which is poured out for you."

As with the first Passover, we remember how on the Cross immediate emancipation followed our acceptance of his gift, we remember his guidance through the wilderness and his providence as we look toward the heavenly Promised Land, the deposit of which dwells in our hearts.

Conclusion

Whether or not you have managed to follow all of this, the crux of the whole thing is this: that the death of Jesus is still relevant, because the agreement between Man and God, foretold of for thousands of years prior, finally instituted on the Cross, stands today and will do until Jesus returns.

Following our individual rejection of God, our route back to him, like the undoing of the work of Adam by Jesus, constitutes a reversal of our original error. In that it is for us now to cast aside our desire for self determination and follow a plan not of our own making but rather of God's making. That plan being the death of Jesus as the single, willing, atoning sacrifice of the son of God for all mankind.

John 14: 6
New International Version (NIV)

Jesus answered, "I am the way and the truth and the life. No one comes to the Father except through me."

The victory of God through the Cross is an eternal victory, the power of which is immeasurably greater than the power of the deception that we once lived under. Two thousand and some years ago it was revealed in time to the world but the Cross is eternal and applicable before, during and after it was unfolded on Calvary. This was how the Israelites were granted forgiveness and also why Jesus and his followers were able to do the miraculous works they did.

John 8:12
New International Version (NIV)

When Jesus spoke again to the people, he said, "I am the light of the world. Whoever follows me will never walk in darkness, but will have the light of life."

John 2:1-11
New International Version (NIV)

On the third day a wedding took place at Cana in Galilee. Jesus' mother was there, and Jesus and his disciples had also been invited to the wedding. When the wine was gone, Jesus' mother said to him, "They have no more wine." "Woman, why do you involve me?" Jesus replied. ""My hour has not yet come." His mother said to the servants, "Do whatever he tells you."

Nearby stood six stone water jars, the kind used by the Jews for ceremonial washing, each holding from twenty to thirty gallons. Jesus said to the servants, "Fill the jars with water"; so they filled them to the brim. Then he told them, "Now draw some out and take it to the master of the banquet."

They did so, and the master of the banquet tasted the water that had been turned into wine. He did not realize where it had come from, though the servants who had drawn the water knew. Then he called the bridegroom aside and said, "Everyone brings out the choice wine first and then the cheaper wine after the guests have had too much to drink; but you have saved the best till now."

What Jesus did here in Cana of Galilee was the first of the signs through which he revealed his glory; and his disciples believed in him.

Notice that at the beginning of his ministry, in full knowledge of his appointed purpose, Jesus fills the jars for cleansing with wine that would become symbolic of his blood. This foreknowledge of his accomplishment was why Jesus was able to make the outlandish statements he made about himself.

This foreknowledge of the Cross was also displayed prior to the Cross in its types. In Jesus Christ it became flesh as God, of himself, brings the Kingdom of Heaven near to all mankind.

Matthew 10: 7-8
New International Version (NIV)

As you go, proclaim this message: 'The kingdom of heaven has come near.' Heal the sick, raise the dead, cleanse those who have leprosy, drive out demons. Freely you have received; freely give.

The Church on Trial: Problems Past and Present

Living in a world where those professing faith in Jesus Christ are responsible for the murder of doctors in the name of a "pro-life" cause (surely the worst contradiction in terms) and where the list of child abuse cases brought against priests and clergy appears to have no limits, it's hardly surprising that cynicism abounds when it comes to the subject of the ability of church going to instil the virtues it so passionately advocates. For me, and no doubt for many still, these failings, and their kin, were good enough reasons to disregard the teachings of Jesus and any idea of taking a closer look at them.

Certainly there are many individuals, organisations and even countries that claim to honour the teachings of Jesus Christ and the Bible, that have more than the odd stain on their garments. Whether it's the Inquisition, the Crusades or more recent history like the Magdalene laundries or phony tele-evangelists, it's clear that not all those calling themselves Christians are necessarily particularly Christ like in their actions.

To get to core of this issue quickly, rather than labouring over specific cases, which I am neither sufficiently studied to discuss nor have the scope for here, the questions we will be addressing here are the substance of what makes these cases an obstacle to enquiry.

The examples of failure that are most commonly brought to the table, like those listed above, as justifications for disregarding the teachings of Jesus Christ, can generally be categorised in one of two groups:

- The failure of individuals to follow the example of Christ.

- The failure of organisations/denominations of the Christian faith to do the same.

It seems to make sense to tackle the problem of the actions of individuals first and then once we gain an insight into this we might save some time looking at the larger issue of the failure of organisations which, after all, are made up of individuals.

Individual Failings

Having parted company with my idyllic childhood surroundings of a country village to find myself a suburb dweller, I would occasionally trail the internet for pictures or news from home. It was on one of these occasions that I came across a disturbing news report telling of how the local Church of England vicar from my quaint village had been charged with possessing indecent images of children on his computer.

The unfortunate yet understandable and obvious result of crimes of this nature being perpetrated by such a person as this, is an immediate discrediting of the Christian witness within the community, which in this instance, I was later to discover, included people known to me who were seeking the counsel of this particular individual at the time.

Firstly, let us be clear that this person's actions are disgraceful and inexcusable, to which he was deservedly held accountable for in a court of law as others who do such things should. The fact that he was a vicar makes no difference, from a biblical standpoint it actually makes it worse: James the brother of Jesus informs us that teachers come under stricter regulations in terms of the Kingdom of God.

James 3: 1
New International Version (NIV)

Not many of you should become teachers, my fellow believers, because you know that we who teach will be judged more strictly.

Rest assured then that I won't, in what follows, be attempting to concoct an elaborate theological excuse for such actions.

Concerning the testimony that these crimes and others like them present us about the teachings of Jesus Christ though, I would hope to look a little deeper than the average pub conversation. The question being not whether or not what this individual and others have done is wrong, but rather: do failings such as this render the message of the Gospel redundant and expose the fallacy of faith?

Even if we don't quite go as far as that, surely if Church leaders are unable to walk the walk then it can't bode well for our own aspirations? What in God's name is going on when a man who was, presumably (given the benefit of the doubt) at some point in his life, committed to the self-sacrificial teachings of Jesus Christ, to then become willingly involved in propagating the most deplorable evil imaginable?

Well we know all action that is contrary to the will of God for our lives, as we discussed in Chapter 3 (The Devil Hell and all that scary stuff), is preceded by our acceptance of the rationale behind the prompting to act, i.e. a person must be open, at least, to the suggestion that there is some benefit to be gained from committing to an act, else there would be no motivation for doing it. So what is going on here? Surely a devout man would be free from being plagued by such moral conflicts? Or is God simply powerless to protect His reputation and the people who represent His kingdom on the earth?

Firstly, despite what we may believe, salvation and church going does not brainwash us into becoming God robots, thus circumventing free will. However, presuming the individual is a genuine recipient of salvation, in the biblical sense of coming into personal relationship with Jesus Christ, there is no excuse for rejecting the will of God a second time: the Bible is very clear on this.

Hebrews 6: 4-6
New International Version (NIV)

It is impossible for those who have once been enlightened, who have tasted the heavenly gift, who have shared in the Holy Spirit, who have tasted the goodness of the word of God and the powers of the coming age and who have fallen away, to be brought back to repentance. To their loss they are crucifying the Son of God all over again and subjecting him to public disgrace.

To further press home the point, one of the scriptures that jumped off the page and became as a hot coal burning in my heart, during the tumultuous times just after accepting Jesus, when I was still ferociously wrestling with the will of the new found presence in my life, was:

2 Peter 2: 20-22
New International Version - UK (NIVUK)

If they have escaped the corruption of the world by knowing our Lord and Saviour Jesus Christ and are again entangled in it and are overcome, they are worse off at the end than they were at the beginning. It would have been better for them not to have known the way of righteousness, than to have known it and then to turn their backs on the sacred command that was passed on to them. Of them the proverbs are true: 'A dog returns to its vomit,' and, 'A sow that is washed returns to her wallowing in the mud.'

For the genuine recipient of salvation by grace, despite there being direct enmity between believers and the pervading spirit of our age, God's hand is upon us to guide our steps and there is no lack of spiritual resources to ward off unwanted attention from the malevolent spiritual forces of the world. Our saviour is our strong tower of protection, while we abide in him, who has subdued and bound the enemy of our souls.

Matthew 12: 27-29
New International Version (NIV)

And if I drive out demons by Beelzebub, by whom do your people drive them out? So then, they will be your judges. But if it is by the Spirit of God that I drive out demons, then the kingdom of God has come upon you.

Or again, how can anyone enter a strong man's house and carry off his possessions unless he first ties up the strong man? Then he can plunder his house.

Nevertheless, in a spiritually hostile world, there are going to be times in a believer's walk with God when the spirit of this world is going to seek them out, to the end of getting them to reconsider to whom and to what their allegiance is pledged. For this reason, Paul, in his letter to the first century Ephesian Church, provides the definitive guide to successfully walking with Jesus through this temporal life. This scripture also highlights much, that I believe, has been neglected by the most commonly recognisable strands of Christian belief in this country, which goes someway to explaining the frequency with which we hear about these failings:

Ephesians 6: 10-18
New International Version (NIV)

Finally, be strong in the Lord and in his mighty power. Put on the full armour of God so that you can take your stand against the devil's schemes. For our struggle is not against flesh and blood, but against the rulers, against the authorities, against the powers of this dark world and against the spiritual forces of evil in the heavenly realms. Therefore put on the full armour of God, so that when the day of evil comes, you may be able to stand your ground, and after you have done everything, to stand. Stand firm then, with the belt of truth buckled around your waist, with the breastplate of righteousness in place, and with your feet fitted with the readiness that comes from the gospel of peace. In addition to all this, take up the shield of faith, with which you can extinguish all the flaming arrows of the evil one. Take the helmet of salvation and the sword of the Spirit, which is the word of God.

And pray in the Spirit on all occasions with all kinds of prayers and requests. With this in mind, be alert and always keep on praying for all the saints.

Concisely provided here, as is always the case in the rare instances that the Bible touches on the subject of the devil, are the answers to how to live victoriously for God. Yet the very first sentence is strikingly at odds with what we are most likely to find in a place of Christian Worship in the UK.

"Be strong in the Lord and in his mighty power!" Paul insists, charging the Church and its members (which are the Church in the original sense of the word) to be channels through which the power of God is manifest in their personal lives and when they congregate for communal worship. Yet the most recognisable strands of the Church in these lands, the Church of England and the Roman Catholic Church, appear to no longer depend upon the power of God, this is most apparent in the fact that they don't encourage their members to seek, as a necessity, a supernatural experience of God; nor do they acknowledge the biblical requirement of a second infilling of the Holy Spirit as a pre-requisite for Christian service; or encourage believers to pursue the supernatural gifts of the spirit clearly outlined in the New Testament. The power of God that Jesus purchased our access to on the Cross appears to have slipped off the programme of these institutions in favour of an adherence to tradition and ritual.

If that weren't trouble enough, the following set of requirements that go hand in hand with being *"strong in God's power"*, summed up by *"putting on the full armour of God"* are again inescapably alien from the culture we are more than likely to come into contact with when visiting a church in this country. Let's take a minute further to unravel a few of Paul's metaphors.

Firstly, he defines the territory of the battle as spiritual, naming the enemy whom we are expected to withstand with the proviso that we have made the following necessary preparations:

The Belt of Truth

Jesus before Pilate counselled his jailer by telling him that all those on the side of truth listened to him. As a cultured Roman, Pilate was no doubt aware of various philosophical arguments and retorted with the rhetorical question "What is truth?" The revelation of the ultimate truth behind our existence and the existence of all we experience is, in no small part, the message of the Gospel. To be effective in our service to God then, there should not be any doubt in this, else perhaps some more time seeking and finding might be required, lest we should enter into this battle with our belt, with all its array of functions for the soldier, unbuckled.

The Breastplate of Righteousness

Another one of those religious words that seems to have no other context for its use in modern times, but to de-religiosify (my own word again), "Righteousness" means to be in right standing with God. To know and learn who we are in God and to maintain our newly reconciled relationship becomes our breastplate. Knowing that we are walking in His will our spiritual heart, through which the love of God overflows to others, is kept safe as is the confidence we have to boldly enter in to God's presence through the frequent communion of our prayers, which is our spiritual breath.

Feet fitted with readiness

The peace in our hearts that comes to us through the message of the Gospel, of having the biggest questions of all resolved and our conscience cleansed, being reconnected to the eternal fountain of joy makes us ready for new challenges and new frontiers.

The Shield of Faith

Faith, put simply, is continuing to put our full trust in the goodness of God and His purposes for our life. The father of faith, Abraham, trusted that God would bless him with a child even though he and his wife were too old and it seemed impossible. The substance of this faith was refusing to doubt the goodness of God in the way Adam and Eve did. Shadrach, Meshach and Abednego, before being thrown in to the fiery furnace, told king Nebuchadnezzar that they knew their God was able to save them from the furnace but even if he didn't they would still not bow to the idol that the King had commanded the people to bow too. It is this 'to the end' faith that extinguishes the fiery arrows of slanderous character accusations of God aimed at our hearts by the enemy.

The Helmet of Salvation

From Paul's metaphor of the helmet of salvation we gain the understanding that without a solid reference point, or appreciation and knowledge of our salvation, our mind and thoughts are vulnerable to the influence of the devil and we will be unable to walk the walk with Christ. The guilt and the persistent reminder of our guilt by the enemy of our soul was the substance of the chains of our bondage that kept us bound. Following the passage of time our old accuser will return again and again and it's helpful to be able to refer him back to the time, date and fact of our salvation in Jesus Christ, when we unconditionally put our lives in his hands.

The Sword of the Spirit

Yet with all these defences should our situation become so dire that we are required to act to repel our accuser then we have also a weapon the words of God. In Genesis we are told that God spoke the world into being, so there is tremendous power in the words of God, and in the Bible we have plenty of ammunition to keep us safe from our adversary. But we must read it, preferably daily, and memorize at least a few verses.

Paul concludes this passage by speaking without metaphor,

encouraging believers to pray continually for one another. It is also clear from his insistence that neglecting any of the aforementioned measures makes us vulnerable. This applies to any believer of any denomination; the true Church is made up of individuals from all denominations, as is the false Church.

However, in terms of the helmet of salvation the fact that those same two most-recognisable strands of the Christian faith make no offer of salvation to their congregations during their weekly service, but rather appear to seek to breed members baptising them with tea and biscuits, or somehow make them Christian by osmosis is doing us no favours whatsoever.

Where is our reference point for the beginning of our old life and the start of our new, when we repented of our former ways and invited God into our hearts ushering in the great change in our lives and the renewal of our souls, if we never make that choice ourselves? Yet Paul is telling us that the fact of our salvation, being able to name the day, the time and the place is the very substance of the metaphorical helmet that protects our mind, and our mind left unguarded in a hostile environment is not going to bode well for us. There is a saying that "God doesn't have any grandchildren", so apologies to anyone who thought otherwise, but the fact that our parents had a vicar splash some water on our head when we were babies doesn't make us right with God. But it is by personally finding God through revelation and choosing to acknowledge the death of Jesus Christ as our personal saviour that brings about a second spiritual birth by the spirit of God, as he comes and dwells within us. Having now accepted and adhered to His plan of salvation we are then found acceptable in is sight.

Although the very tone of Paul's words bears little resemblance to the manner of any message you are likely to hear from a pulpit in this country, we might ask: despite our many technological advances, has the spiritual character of our world changed so greatly that it ought to warrant such a grand re-appraisal of our standing?

In fact, if we view our position in time from a biblical standpoint it would make a lot more sense to assume that the fight today would be more intense than in the first century when the preceding scripture was written. Given that God has decreed an end to the current state of proceedings, in the prophesied return of Jesus Christ that will right the wrongs done upon the Earth. Although he is keeping the precise date to himself, the one thing the current ruler in the world knows is that each passing day draws his doom that bit closer, making the struggle ever more intense as time for the return of Jesus approaches.

1 Peter 5: 8
New International Version (NIV)

Be self-controlled and alert. Your enemy the devil prowls around like a roaring lion looking for someone to devour.

Taking on a position of leadership in the Church, you need to be fully equipped as you are singling yourself out as representative of the only true God. Given that the Devil's days are numbered and his resources limited, strategically the deception of a member of the congregation may mean one less person in church but the deception of their leader is a much more attractive prospect, that may mean one less congregation. Not to mention the press.

A vicar, worn-out, slack, complacent, or even better, one who doesn't truthfully know God for himself, would be an ideal target for a prowling devourer seeking to discredit the reputation of God.

As outside of the knowledge of Jesus Christ, more often than not, these failings are seen by the majority as simply another flaw in a fallen God that we don't believe in anyway, rather than the reality of them being simply another example of fallen man failing to fulfil his purpose as God's earthly representative, in which there is nothing new at all.

The testimony we ought to be reading about and studying if we are enquiring after the God of the Bible is the testimony left by God himself through His son Jesus Christ, who lives that we may find our faith in God upon him and him alone. The works and person of

Jesus Christ as set before us in the Bible, and the revelation of their truth deposited in our hearts by the Holy Spirit, is the rock upon which our walk of faith is founded and remains throughout. This is why Hebrews refers to him in his as the "author and finisher of our faith" as it is him who draws us out of the world, him who guides us throughout our walk with him and he who will be there at the end of life's journey.

Hebrews 12: 2
New King James Version (NKJV)

...looking unto Jesus, the author and finisher of our faith, who for the joy that was set before Him endured the cross, despising the shame, and has sat down at the right hand of the throne of God.

If every person who claimed to be born of God adhered to the teachings of Jesus and walked as Jesus did as the first believers clearly did, so much so that the world nick-named them "Christians", then the world may be able to see more plainly the "light of the world", which is something that the body of Christ needs to work on. But we are just the body; he is the head and leader of his Church. Church ought not to be viewed as this twee social club of goody two shoes where one bad apple spoils the whole.

Rather, be encouraged to get to know the living Jesus and find out if he is worth following. Find a good Church and pray for your Church leaders that they may honour God with their lives.

Collective Failings

As much a disservice the testimony of these backslidden, disingenuous or misinformed individuals does to the Gospel of truth, perhaps a greater disservice is done by the collective crimes and criminal policies of organisations who claim to represent Jesus Christ on the earth. This cannot be explained as easily as one or two wilfully corrupted individuals as it requires the compliance of the whole!

So how is it that an organisation claiming to represent the will of God on the earth, and professing to be acting in accordance with the will of Jesus Christ, as laid out in the Bible, can manage to repeatedly sustain policies of action for years which are fundamentally cruel?

Without pointing the finger too directly at any particular organisation, what are the collective failings most readily associated with Christian religious institutions?

> Greed = Yes
> Exploitation of the poor and needy = Yes
> Distortion of the Christian message to further their own ends = Yes
> Lack of compassion, i.e. cruelty = Yep
> Psychological enslavement = Yep
> Alignment with unjust military causes/questionable political leaders = Yes

It's inconceivable to imagine that an organisation that is truly founded on and is consistently adhering to the singular truth of a loving God, the creator of the universe, could possibly be even compliant in the kinds of activities listed above, let alone be the orchestrator. So how is it that the history of Christian institutions is so blotted with all of the above and more?

Seemingly barring our path to this problem, however, is the following conundrum: if we are using the Bible as the final word from God on all things and our guide in these matters and seeing then that the organised Christian faith in its present form, and its crimes, are post the Bible, then where exactly are we supposed to turn to understand the heart of God in relation to these matters?

Are we simply left in the dark to rely on our own fallible moral reasoning? Or does this God simply side with the opinion of anyone who wears a funny shaped hat, priestly robes and carries a crook?

Well the God of the Bible declares that He is the "Alpha and Omega, the beginning and the end", which means He stands outside of time and is aware of all the issues that mankind yesterday, today and tomorrow has and will face.

Revelation 22:13
New International Version (NIV)

I am the Alpha and the Omega, the First and the Last, the Beginning and the End.

As such, He is able to pick and choose the right time in history to send His son to earth to save mankind. We can therefore be assured that the Bible as a spiritual history of the human race deals with all the issues of the human condition and leaves nothing out.

With all our rapidly advancing technology, in our arrogance we can easily become conceited believing we have entered into times which the biblical world could not have conceived of. Yet our arrogance is unfounded as the Bible contains many descriptions in prophesy of the character and events of our times as we observed briefly in Chapter 4 (The Authenticity of the Bible).

The ingenuity of mankind, although taking the historical Church by surprise from time to time, holds no surprises for God. Isaiah

describes the Earth as circular thousands of years before this became common knowledge or accepted by the established church.

Isaiah 40: 22
New International Version (NIV)

He sits enthroned above the circle of the earth,
   and its people are like grasshoppers.
He stretches out the heavens like a canopy,
   and spreads them out like a tent to live in.

It has been noted that the timing of the appearance of Jesus Christ and the Gospel was incredibly advantageous for several reasons: the Jewish people, who knew God better than any through the Laws of Moses, were dispersed throughout the Mediterranean in search of riches, the Greek language had become universally spoken, plus the Romans had built roads enabling ease of passage for missionaries. Let us also remind ourselves again that Jesus declared that, although his external surroundings may change, Man for the time being would remain in essence the same until his return, meaning that today's Churches are equally capable of repeating the mistakes of their biblical predecessors.

Luke 21:32
New International Version (NIV)

"Truly I tell you, this generation will certainly not pass away until all these things have happened".

So let us look at how the religious institutions of Jesus' time fared and what his assessment of them was and see if there are any parallels with the complaints voiced in our times. (If you have a vested interest in this chapter due to some personal grievance with a Church organisation then I hope what follows will offer some comfort.)

The first rebuke of the ruling religious class in the Gospels in fact comes not from Jesus but from John the Baptist. Because of the signs that accompanied his birth and the subsequent success of his prophetic ministry, the religious leaders sent emissaries to enquire into the nature of John's work. Rather than John regarding their presence as an affirmation of the legitimacy of his work, he publically rebukes them whilst confirming that the institution itself had exchanged its original position for one that was no longer connected to God:

Matthew 3 7:10
New International Version (NIV)

But when he saw many of the Pharisees and Sadducees coming to where he was baptizing, he said to them: "You brood of vipers! Who warned you to flee from the coming wrath? Produce fruit in keeping with repentance. And do not think you can say to yourselves, 'We have Abraham as our father.' I tell you that out of these stones God can raise up children for Abraham. The axe is already at the root of the trees, and every tree that does not produce good fruit will be cut down and thrown into the fire.

Greed

With regards to greed, Jesus directly states this as a character weakness of the religious leaders of his time, going as far as to refer to greed as their master. The parable found in *Luke 16: 1-14* describes the twisted relationship between the master greed and the stewards, the Pharisees, which concludes with this damning indictment of their position:

Luke 16:13
New International Version (NIV)

"No one can serve two masters. Either you will hate the one and love the other, or you will be devoted to the one and despise the other. You cannot serve both God and money."

Basically a greedy person cannot be a servant or representative of God, the two just don't go together! Yet not only was this a characteristic of their personality it was also the motivation for instituting traditions such as selling sacrificial doves and other religious merchandise in the temple courts. The reaction of Jesus to this is well known, but the point often overlooked is that Jesus' anger stems from the corruption of the temple as a refuge for the poor and the needy, into a worship place of greed.

Exploitation of the poor and needy

The exploitation of the poor and needy, particularly widows, brings upon the Pharisees and Scribes perhaps the harshest judgement of their role by Jesus:

Luke 12: 35-40
New International Version (NIV)

As he taught, Jesus said, "Watch out for the teachers of the law. They like to walk around in flowing robes and be greeted with respect in the marketplaces, and have the most important seats in the synagogues and the places of honour at banquets. They devour widows' houses and for a show make lengthy prayers. These men will be punished most severely."

We have to bear in mind here the patriarchal (male dominated) nature of the society of the time and the vulnerability of a woman widowed with all her husband's affairs to put in order. Whilst also trying to come to terms with how to provide for herself and her family in the future, a widow would often turn to the literate Scribes and Pharisees who were familiar with the officialdom of the time. Their crime however, that warranted such severe judgement from the Lord, was of abusing their position of trust to defraud the weak and vulnerable, using long prayers, the wearing of robes and the very truth of God as a mask of religious piety in service of personal gain, even despite David, the major hero of Jewish tradition, already declaring that God upholds the widow and the fatherless.

Psalm 146: 9
New International Version (NIV)

The Lord watches over the foreigner
and sustains the fatherless and the widow,
but he frustrates the ways of the wicked.

The extremity of the rebuke, in the previous passage from Luke, is then due not only because of the crime itself but also due to the defaming of the truth of God. Religious leaders today who engage in such activity should not expect Jesus to be any more lenient.

Distortion of the Christian message to further their own ends

Money was such an overwhelming obsession of the Pharisees that they were even prepared to invent traditions that contradicted the teaching of God. Such a ruling is exposed by Jesus in the Gospel of Matthew.

Matthew 15: 4-6
Amplified Bible (AMP)

For God commanded, Honour your father and your mother, and, He who curses or reviles or speaks evil of or abuses or treats improperly his father or mother, let him surely come to his end by death.

But you say, If anyone tells his father or mother, What you would have gained from me [that is, the money and whatever I have that might be used for helping you] is already dedicated as a gift to God, then he is exempt and no longer under obligation to honour and help his father or his mother.

So for the sake of your tradition (the rules handed down by your forefathers), you have set aside the Word of God [depriving it of force and authority and making it of no effect].

No, the Pharisees were not averse to bending a few scriptures, if it meant that they were going to be the financial beneficiaries. I have provided the translation here from the Amplified Bible as it gives us a clearer understanding of the Pharisees' disregard, or irreverence, for the recorded words of God, which fuelled their corruption.

Lack of compassion

With regards to an absence of compassion in the Church, this is in essence the source of the anger which led Jesus to turn the tables in the temple over. The sanctuary of God ought to be available for people of all nations to seek the face of God in their hour of need. In addition, James, the brother of Jesus, tells us that in the new covenant of the Gospel "mercy triumphs over judgement". Yet how many are cut off from seeking the face of God and receiving the blessings found in his presence today due to the unsanctioned judgemental attitude, and unwelcoming nature of some Churches?

James also tells us that religion that is acceptable to God is "caring for orphans and widows". Yet the history of some organisations would suggest that they misinterpreted this recommendation as an order to increase the numbers of both!

Jesus himself sought out those who, even by worldly standards, were wretched to remind us that where we see hopelessness God sees an opportunity to provide a testimony of the transforming power of his love.

Psychological enslavement

The Gospel message that Jesus preached was one of freedom and liberty. Freedom from the oppression of Satan's monologue of accusations and the resulting dissipation of the life of our souls caused by our separation from the fountain of life, our heavenly father. In his very first public speech Jesus read:

Isaiah 61: 1
New International Version (NIV)

"The Spirit of the Lord is on me,
   because he has anointed me
   to proclaim good news to the poor.
He has sent me to proclaim freedom for the prisoners
   and recovery of sight for the blind,
to set the oppressed free,
   to proclaim the year of the Lord's favour."

Yet many see affiliation to the Christian teachings as akin to donning a straight jacket. So how has the Gospel of liberty come to be purveyed as an unnecessarily torturous straight jacket of rules and regulations that only the incredibly dedicated are able to maintain? Strange, as Jesus in fact instituted very few rituals that he wished his followers to observe, the breaking of bread and drinking of wine known as the Lord's Supper and the washing of the Saints Feet are the only outlined in the Bible.

When ministering in the famous discourse with the Samaritan "woman at the well" Jesus declares that his future worshippers shall worship not in any particular location but in "spirit and in truth". So how did being holy get so complicated?

In the days of the Pharisees it was, as it is today, tradition and the upkeep of traditions that complicated matters. Yet Jesus reveals below that those who knew the requirements of God for themselves in his day were unwilling to expend their own energy to uphold the traditions of their forefathers, but were more than happy for their subjects to.

Luke 11: 46
New International Version (NIV)

Jesus replied, "And you experts in the law, woe to you, because you load people down with burdens they can hardly carry, and you yourselves will not lift one finger to help them..."

The problem with man-made tradition is that it walks hand in hand with stagnation and death. Which is okay if that's the kind of God you're following, but the God of the Bible is a God of life who creates a different sunset each evening; no two ever the same and creates every person unique. So when John appeared in the desert proclaiming the coming of the kingdom of God, drawing the multitudes to him, the traditionalists with their carefully thought out rituals, entrenched over generations, were unable to respond to this new move of God. As a result, they cut themselves off from the blessing of God. Then, with the fulfilment of John's preaching appearing in Jesus and destruction of their treasured traditions threatened, having exalted tradition rather than the truth of God, they used their influence to intimidate every earnest soul who would dare cast a glance toward the place where the Spirit of God is active and the revelation of God is found.

Luke 11: 52
New International Version (NIV)

"Woe to you experts in the law, because you have taken away the key to knowledge. You yourselves have not entered, and you have hindered those who were entering."

If you personally are affected by some misleading teaching or misinterpretation of the Bible, I would recommend that you look it up for yourself first and pray about it earnestly. Tempting Jesus in the desert, Satan twice misquotes scripture; he is still at it today and it is he, not Jesus, who has a wardrobe full of sleeveless jackets!

Alignment with unjust military causes/questionable political leaders

One of the most recent changes in the public mood, with regards to this country and the validity of its foundation in Christian beliefs, was its involvement in hugely unpopular military campaigns overseas. Although we generally see ourselves and our governments as secular, the novelty of these campaigns was that the figureheads of both parties involved professed to be practising Christians, with one leader even quoted as saying that he believed he was doing God's will by sanctioning military action. The world however was, with good reason, suspicious that the motives were rather less profound and more to do with the West's reliance on the number one commodity on the world stock exchange: that of oil. As far as the world's view of the Christian teaching was concerned, linking Christians to a questionably motivated conflict in which innocents would pay the ultimate price was a clear witness to the moral bankruptcy of the Church's teachings. As the years pass, and the number of soldiers from these shores that return dead rises, there is a collective sadness for the loss but still a shadow over the nobility of the cause leaving us in a kind of moral no man's land.

So where does this leave us on the question of accepting the authority of Jesus Christ over our lives? If we sign up, are we simply expected to fall in-line behind our leaders and offer them our unwavering support?

Firstly, these leaders as dedicated as they may profess to be, are political leaders who happen to claim to be religious, and not themselves religious leaders. In light of this, disavowing fellowship to a particular teaching based on their behaviour would be rejecting Jesus on the basis of an individual's inability to follow his teaching and example, which we covered in the previous chapter.

The basic question that is being posed to us in amongst all this is: as a follower of Christ, where ought our worldly political allegiances to lie? To whom's banner ought we to tie our colours too. The same question was asked of Jesus in the temple in an attempt by the Jewish teachers to catch Jesus out in his words and make him unpopular with the crowds who were becoming increasingly enamoured with his teaching, but passionately opposed the Roman occupation of their lands. The scripture goes as follows:

Luke 20 20:26
New International Version (NIV)

Keeping a close watch on him, they sent spies, who pretended to be sincere. They hoped to catch Jesus in something he said, so that they might hand him over to the power and authority of the governor. So the spies questioned him: "Teacher, we know that you speak and teach what is right, and that you do not show partiality but teach the way of God in accordance with the truth. Is it right for us to pay taxes to Caesar or not?"

He saw through their duplicity and said to them, "Show me a denarius. Whose image and inscription are on it?"

"Caesar's," they replied.

He said to them, "Then give back to Caesar what is Caesar's, and to God what is God's."

They were unable to trap him in what he had said there in public. And astonished by his answer, they became silent.

What is emphasized by Jesus is that in the midst all this human conflict, if we are to make sense of anything, we must get first things first and take hold of the only citizenship that matters, that of God's kingdom. Once we are assured of our citizenship through accepting Jesus Christ as the authority over our life, and our guide, then we can begin to address the pertinent issues of the world and seek God's guidance as to where, or in what role, we may be most effective for God in bringing about His will on the earth. One of our main forms of worship is the use of our earthly time to His service. In His kingdom, and in His will, we become part of the solution to the ending of all wars and suffering through the furtherance of His kingdom amongst men.

Now it is possible that God may call us to political activism or to fight against political injustice in one form or another and in God's will we can be assured of success, but equally venturing outside of God's purposes for our lives, preferring endeavours of our own choosing is rebellion from which we can only add further confusion to an already confusing world.

God is by no means unconcerned about the suffering and injustice in the world, but through a restored relationship with Him we become involved in His mission and His cause which is far more pressing than any earthly conflict; that of the struggle to win the eternal souls of mankind to God, in doing so tackling the root cause of all wars.

Although many of us are keen to set the world to rights over a coffee or something a bit stronger, who amongst us truly envies the position of our leaders?! I do not have all the answers and my calling is not to a life in politics, but I know Jesus is the truth and I know that God is a God of justice who protects and preserves the innocent, so if our leaders are professing to know Him then they ought to be wary of His judgement should their motives be less than honourable.

John 9: 41
New International Version (NIV)

Jesus said, "If you were blind, you would not be guilty of sin; but now that you claim you can see, your guilt remains".

Encouraged by a growing knowledge and experience of God and His word, as we take on God's purposes for our lives, it becomes possible for the believer to confidently entrust our concerns about our world to God in prayer with heartfelt petition, knowing that the God of heaven hears and answers prayer and unlike the people of

Jesus' time under Roman occupation we have the option of changing our government via the ballot box.

Although proposals of this nature are unlikely to quell the righteous indignation of those as horrified as we all are by the suffering of innocents, or their desire to see radical action taken. We would do well to be reminded that doing what the Bible says was radical enough to take the teachings of a Jewish carpenter all over the world; to bring down one of the cruellest empires in history, the Roman Empire, and become the foundation of the most stable and peaceful democratic nations in the world. It is radical enough for the Bible still to be banned in certain parts of the world and radical enough to usher in a new age of righteousness in this country if we want it.

Should anyone share my own political sensitivities, a final word on an issue that was foremost in my own personal journey of faith, namely the situation in the middle-east, particularly with regards to Israel and Palestine. It is clear that neither side has particularly covered themselves in glory, yet what you won't get from the news, but you will get with a little research and a bit of exposure to the

Arab world, is an awareness of the rich vein of anti-Jewish sentiment found there which has its foundation in the religious beliefs of these peoples.

In 1937, King Saud told Colonel H.R.P. Dickson:

Today we and our subjects are deeply troubled over this Palestine question, and the cause of our disquiet and anxiety is the strange attitude of your British Government, and the still more strange hypnotic influence which the Jews, a race accursed by God according to His Holy Book, and destined to final destruction and eternal damnation hereafter, appear to wield over them and the English people generally

That one I will leave with you for now.

I hope the common complaints I listed at the start of this section have been addressed sufficiently enough to at least warrant our own considered reappraisal of such matters. Unsurprisingly, all that is lacking within Christendom has roots not in the fallibility of God but rather in Man's fallibility in representing Him adequately in the world. The Church (however you want to define that), even organisations that are truly populated by individuals called by God, are still made up of men and liable to some degree of error.

Stumbling and fallible as the Church is, only the fiercest opposition would even attempt to argue against the multitude of benefits and liberties we take for granted in today's society that simply wouldn't exist if it weren't for the organised Christian faith and its adherents. All the celebrated major reforms in British society that we are so proud of were brought about by a country that had devout men in spheres of influence and a Christianised conscience. Still today 90% of all non-government sponsored aid comes from Christian organisations. Improvement is undoubtedly needed if it is to become the spotless bride described in Revelation, rising to meet Jesus on his return, but what the Church doesn't need is more people standing at a distance wagging their finger. If the Church is full of bad people then how about we even up the numbers a bit by adding our names to the membership and bring the Church closer to God from within, rather than standing on the outside waiting for the Church to become as righteous as we suppose we are?

Women and the Bible

Bolstered by the popularization of the modern myth of a romantic relationship between Jesus and Mary Magdalene, much has been made in recent years of the supposed erasing of the contribution of women in the Bible. Personally, the attitude of Jesus towards women never invoked the indignation other aspects of biblical teaching did, however when I got into the Old Testament and the Epistles I found plenty of eyebrow raising material! In no small part though, the subject of Women in the Bible became a pertinent issue in our house due to my wife, so this chapter will hopefully serve to placate the concerns of anyone with similar convictions.

What I am hoping is that, in the course of this chapter, we can encourage the sceptic that there is no need for such a restoration of the role of women in the work of God as the aforementioned myths that create bestsellers and hit films propose. Taking examples from different sections of scripture we will see, hopefully, that far from devaluing women, the Bible holds women as central to the purposes of God and the underlying motives of such myths will no doubt be revealed as predictably familiar.

What I won't be addressing is the abuses of women by various church organisations, the root causes of which I endeavoured to tackle in the previous chapter. Our understanding will be gleamed, as with all of the previous chapters, from the recorded words of Jesus himself in the Gospels, the scriptures which he believed and quoted, i.e. the Old Testament, and the writings of those closest to him.

Okay let's get started. Firstly we need to overcome the basic yet important point that most translations of the Bible use the word "man" where "mankind" or "humankind" would equally suffice. So we can be encouraged immediately that the Bible is not concerned solely with one half of the world's population!

The beginning is usually a good place to start and, in this case, Genesis presents us with an array of scriptures each with a multitude of misconceptions and misrepresentations about the heart of God with regards to women. Let's start with the first, and possibly the scripture most commonly attributed to the biblical devaluing of women, that of the Creation.

Genesis 2: 20-24
New International Version (NIV)

So the man gave names to all the livestock, the birds in the sky and all the wild animals.

But for Adam no suitable helper was found. So the Lord God caused the man to fall into a deep sleep; and while he was sleeping, he took one of the man's ribs and then closed up the place with flesh. Then the Lord God made a woman from the rib he had taken out of the man, and he brought her to the man.

The man said,

"This is now bone of my bones
 and flesh of my flesh;
 she shall be called 'woman,'
 for she was taken out of man."

That is why a man leaves his father and mother and is united to his wife, and they become one flesh.

We have actually been over part of this scripture already when we talked about how the Bible was primarily a spiritual book. With this understanding in place (*please recap if you have forgotten from the chapter "The Bible and sex"*) we know that primarily we are talking about spiritual qualities being removed from man. So in this context, to use a colloquial phrase, the scripture is telling us that woman truly has become man's "other half", literally embodying qualities that man does not possess. Equally then it follows that man also possesses qualities not found in woman.

Much of the understanding and misconceived notions about the Bible's attitudes towards women hinge on this teaching. The world's version of equality says that women and men must be treated with equal respect and therefore they must be treated as equal in every aspect of life so we mustn't say that men are generally better than this and women are overall better at that, because that is sexist and discriminatory. The Bible however attributes different spiritual qualities to each, whilst acknowledging both warrant equal respect as children of God.

But hang on, didn't we just read in the preceding scripture that woman is the man's helper; His subordinate; His servant; His slave? Well actually no, this happens to be an unfortunate compromise of the translation process in that there aren't always English words that correspond exactly to the original meaning of the text. The word translated here as helper is "ezer" which is actually used in the Hebrew to describe a superior being. Elsewhere in the Bible the same word is used in such context as *"My help comes from the Lord the maker of heaven and earth"* in *Psalm 121: 2.* Also it is found in *Exodus 18: 4* were Moses names his son Eliezer meaning God is my helper, exclaiming *"My father's God was my helper; he saved me from the sword of Pharaoh."* There are other examples but you get the idea. Woman was not created to be man's servant.

It has been suggested that the nature and timing of the creation of Adam, and subsequently Eve, has also a recognisable spiritual inheritance in that Man was created with a position in God's creation without relationship to any of his own kind, whereas woman was created into relationship. So commonly today we find that women are more interested in establishing the relational connections when confronted with strangers, whereas men will more regularly ask each other what they do for a living, therefore establishing their role or position first.

This may well have been the reason that Satan approached Eve rather than Adam, as Adam would be keener to establish the stranger's position before entertaining him in conversation. As it was, Eve was the first deceived by the serpent or "shining one" and then led Adam down the same path of rebellion.

Yet curiously in the disciplining of the unrepentant pair, Adam is the one who is held responsible: why?

Following the sequence of events, we see that Adam is given the instruction relating to the tree before Eve was created. Although the message had clearly made its way to Eve, as she quotes the instruction in conversation to the inquisitive stranger, the message obviously hadn't really been communicated effectively enough. Perhaps because, as is shown by Adam's willing compliance in the folly, that he also was failing to grasp the importance of the command. The bottom line for God was that this was his jurisdiction and therefore it was he who was directly culpable and secondly Eve.

It is this scenario that provides the basis for the roles attributed within Christian families where, in acknowledgement that the man is to be held responsible by God for the effectiveness of his proliferation of the teachings of God, he is granted the role of spiritual leader. A blessing, however, that also charges the man, 'to love his wife as Jesus loved the church', in other words to give his everything to God for her sake so that his love would be so irrepressible that it would overcome all her fears. Many of us admittedly are still working on this one.

Ephesians 5: 25
New International Version (NIV)

Husbands, love your wives, just as Christ loved the church and gave himself up for her...

After being banished from the garden, Man is told that he will: "eat by the sweat of his brow" until he returns to the ground from which he was made. Eve is told that she will experience increased sorrow in child birth, yet this will not counteract the command to increase and be fruitful, so the woman will nevertheless continue to desire to be with man who will rule over her!

If the last scripture sounded bad then this sounds worse! Before we become too indignant though, we need to be mindful not to fall into the same trap as those we are discussing and doubt the loving nature of God. For this is the central theme of all the stories of the heroes of faith.

The actual scripture reads as follows:

Genesis 3: 16
New International Version (NIV)

Unto the woman he said, I will greatly multiply thy sorrow and thy conception; in sorrow thou shalt bring forth children; and thy desire shall be to thy husband, and he shall rule over thee.

I have used the translation from the King James Version because of the choice of the word "sorrow" instead of the other rather numerous possibilities, such as "pain", "hurt", "toil", "labour", or "hardship", as it makes more sense, especially in the context of the whole story's unnervingly accurate description of the spiritual attitude of the heart of mankind.

In the fallen world of war and strife that followed Adam and Eve's rebellion, with children bound to repeat the folly of their forefathers whilst adding new follies all their own, women (speaking of all women following Eve), giving birth to beautiful innocent children full of the light of God shining out of their eyes, are bound to experience an "increase" of their "sorrows" as compared to raising children in the paradise of Eden, where evil was literally unheard of. Truly in our day such is the fear of bringing children into this world in our own time that many take drastic measures, multiplying their own sorrows, to keep their children from it!

The declaration that "man would rule over woman" has a similar but more obvious practical explanation. Following the rebellion of humankind man (due to his physical superiority and the fact that he doesn't bear children) would inevitably become the ruler of the power hungry, self-centred world that would ensue.

God, here is not issuing a decree then, but is rather informing them of the outcome of their chosen course of action. As the children of Israel were offered a choice about their future when entering into the promised land of either the blessings of being faithful to their creator or the curses that would come upon them as a result of their unfaithfulness, should they turn from following him, so Adam and Eve faced the same choice, with the same God, and despite being warned followed their own path regardless.

Deuteronomy 11: 26-28
New International Version (NIV)

See, I am setting before you today a blessing and a curse the blessing if you obey the commands of the Lord your God that I am giving you today; the curse if you disobey the commands of the Lord your God and turn from the way that I command you today by following other gods, which you have not known.

Further to what we have already discussed from the Creation story is the promise that, in addition to becoming the mother of humanity, womankind would be the vessel through which God himself would descend to earth to crush the head of the serpent (silencing his lying tongue) and redeem His lost special creation. This was fulfilled dramatically through the Bible's main female heroine Mary the mother of Jesus.

Hopefully we are beginning to see now that in God's plan woman was never intended to play second fiddle to man, as she has done for much of human history and still does today in many places. But rather this became the case in much of the world as a result of humankind's rejection of God.

Fast forward to the times of the Old Testament and we see the world of fallen humanity in full swing where women, despite the few exceptions, are completely dependent on, and in subjection to, men to the extent that wives and daughters are seen as little more than slaves. Oh yes, by now we have invented slavery too.

There are many difficult texts in the Old Testament for women, especially within the Laws of Moses, which appear hard to reconcile with the understanding of a loving creator. Before we attempt to appropriate these scriptures, there are a few things we need to understand about the work God was and is doing among his people.

Firstly, we need to understand the state of the peoples of that time in that part of the world. For example, the Bible explains that while the Israelites were kept as slaves in Egypt the current occupants of the Promised Land were being given the opportunity to change. But by the time the Israelites appeared on their doorstep the crimes of the prior inhabitants of Israel had become so beyond redemption that God was required to act. To give you an idea, these were nations where child massacres, rape, prostitution, and mutilation were not merely occurring but had become part of standard religious practise!!!

Leviticus 18: 21
New International Version (NIV)

"Do not give any of your children to be sacrificed to Molek, for you must not profane the name of your God. I am the Lord".

The modern day reference I keep returning to that helps me grasp the gravity of the depraved nature of such societies is the culture depicted in the popular 80s film, Indiana Jones and the Temple of Doom, where a secret community are continuing to offer human sacrifices deep underground while child slaves fund it all by working in mines.

Following the flood, God had promised that a "back to the drawing board" approach to man's failings was off the table; instead God would reveal His power and authority to the world through a people. Not just any people either but the smallest and least known of the peoples of the earth: the Hebrews. Embittered, degraded and broken in every way; slaves under the rule of by far and away the greatest most powerful force in the world at that time; the builders of monuments that people thousands of years on would travel from the ends of the earth of to marvel at; a people of great and lasting reputation from out of whose hands God would set His chosen bedraggled people free and have them record it so that His sovereign power may be known to all.

After God displayed His authority by freeing the Hebrews from Egypt and Pharaoh, He proceeds to put in place His plan to take this "least of people", this nation of downtrodden nobody's, and reform them to become His representatives on the earth and a light to all the nations of the world.

(Note: Israel is located in what is known as the crossroads of the ancient world, where all the ancient trading routes converged.)

However, this would be a process rather than an overnight job. Consequently, in His early dealings with His people He granted them, for a season, concessions with regards to their behaviour allowing many cultural norms of the time to continue, including the role and status of women. Jesus affirms this idea of temporary concession in his teachings on the Laws of Moses pertaining to divorce:

Matthew 19: 3-8
New International Version (NIV)

Some Pharisees came to him to test him. They asked, "Is it lawful for a man to divorce his wife for any and every reason?"

"Haven't you read," he replied, "that at the beginning the Creator 'made them male and female,' and said, 'For this reason a man will leave his father and mother and be united to his wife, and the two will become one flesh'? So they are no longer two, but one flesh. Therefore what God has joined together, let no one separate."

"Why then," they asked, "did Moses command that a man give his wife a certificate of divorce and send her away?"

Jesus replied, "Moses permitted you to divorce your wives because your hearts were hard. But it was not this way from the beginning".

So in terms of the original regulations of Moses we can be assured that they include these temporary concessions, that we now find offensive, but which were allowed to continue until the reformation of the people and the culture made such practises no longer acceptable.

Nevertheless, the Old Testament is not all doom and gloom when it comes to the subject of women. The poetic language used in the Old Testament reveres woman in using expression such as "The daughter of Zion" and referring to his people as his bride. Along with the aforementioned exceptions to the rule, the Old Testament has three books named after female heroes of faith and contains many others. The first the book of Deborah is named after one of thirteen female prophetesses in the Old Testament and the only woman Judge of thirteen who led Israel in the 300 or so years between the death of Joshua, who took over from Moses, and Saul the first king of Israel who was eventually succeeded by King David. Judges were valiant and courageous individuals who would appear in Israel's hour of need, when the people would cry out to God because of the oppression of their enemies round about, to lead the people into God's plan for their deliverance. The recurring precursor to these deliverances was the rebellion of the Jewish people and their rejection of God in favour of idols. Of all the

Judges, Deborah is regarded as possibly the best as she didn't display the hesitancy and weaknesses of other male Judges of whose ministry we have an account.

In the same time period we have the mini soap opera that is the book of Ruth which tells not only of the heavenly virtue found within a woman but also of the virtue of a non-Hebrew woman who was only associated to the Israelites by her dead husband, yet through her faithfulness becomes the great grandmother of King David and part of the human ancestry of Christ. Although short, this book is rich in meaning and at its heart is a foretelling of the coming of Jesus.

The book of Esther tells of the faithfulness of God to the promise he made to Abraham thousands of years earlier when He said that He would "bless those that bless Him and curse those who curse Him". The story is set amongst the Jewish people taken captive by the Babylonians now under the rule of the Persians, who had not returned to Jerusalem following their release by King Darius.

Genesis 12: 3
New International Version (NIV)

"I will bless those who bless you,
*   and whoever curses you I will curse;*
and all peoples on earth
*   will be blessed through you."*

Under threat from the Prime Minister of the time, Queen Esther, as an instrument of God, uses her position and influence to secure the continued freedom and safety of a Jewish people on the brink of annihilation and the destruction of their oppressor.

The greatest reformer of all, of course, was Jesus Christ, the physical embodiment of God's will for humanity. The scripture above where Jesus talks about divorce, for the time, was revolutionary. Insisting that husbands take full responsibility for their wives for the duration of their lives, bearing in mind the complete reliance of women upon men in the male dominated society where women were not even provided with an education and divorce was more akin to abandonment, was a reprimand for men yet full of mercy for women. Marriage was also used symbolically to represent Jesus' relationship to his Church; hence Jesus' insistence on men not rejecting their wives to the corruption of the world.

Jesus managed to not only to reform attitudes towards divorce but to go on, and out of his way, to completely shatter every discriminatory cultural prejudice/taboo of his time and usher in a revolution with regards to the role of women in society.

To give a few examples:

Firstly, "many women" were among his followers and part of his inner circle where previously the priestly office was a strictly male domain like most else. Such was the devotion of these women that it is worthwhile to note that it was they who were last to leave the cross at Calvary and it was they who were first to the tomb on the Sunday of his resurrection, where it was to Mary Magdalene he first appeared, entrusting to her the task of witnessing to the other Disciples of his triumph over death in a time and place where the testimony of a woman was not accepted in a court of law!

In addition, when speaking of women, he referred to them as daughters of Abraham. He broke racial barriers and social taboos by individually ministering to the Samaritan woman at the well: Jews were not supposed to mix with the "unclean" Samaritan people, neither was it socially acceptable for a man to approach a woman in a public place and start a conversation.

John 4: 9
New International Version (NIV)

The Samaritan woman said to him, "You are a Jew and I am a

*Samaritan woman. How can you ask me for a drink?" (For Jews do
not associate with Samaritans.)*

As we noted in an earlier chapter (The church on trial crimes past
and present), Jesus championed the cause of widows, condemning
their exploitation by the male religious elite.

Whereas Jewish law demanded that adulterers be put to death by
stoning, Jesus in one of the most memorable acts of his ministry
takes up the case of Mary Magdalene, a woman of dubious
reputation caught in the very act. He rebukes her accusers and
exposing their hypocrisy with regards to their appearance of
righteousness.

John 8: 3-11
New International Version (NIV)

*The teachers of the law and the Pharisees brought in a woman
caught in adultery. They made her stand before the group and
said to Jesus, "Teacher, this woman was caught in the act of
adultery. In the Law Moses commanded us to stone such
women. Now what do you say?" They were using this question as
a trap, in order to have a basis for accusing him.*

*But Jesus bent down and started to write on the ground with his
finger. When they kept on questioning him, he straightened up
and said to them, "Let any one of you who is without sin be the
first to throw a stone at her." Again he stooped down and wrote
on the ground.*

*At this, those who heard began to go away one at a time, the
older ones first, until only Jesus was left, with the woman still
standing there. Jesus straightened up and asked her, "Woman,*

where are they? Has no one condemned you?"

"No one, sir," she said.

"Then neither do I condemn you," Jesus declared. "Go now and leave your life of sin."

Equally, Jesus rebukes the condescension of his host towards the woman who washed his feet with her tears, exalting her for her great love for him in *Luke 7: 38*. As he did also to the woman with the alabaster jar who anointed him with expensive perfume on the evening before he was due to suffer in *Matthew 26: 7*.

Disregarding ritual purification, Jesus bestows praise upon the woman with the issue of blood, who forces her way through the throng of people to touch the hem of Jesus' garment, declaring that her "faith made her whole" in *Mark 5: 25*, but also appears in Matthew and Luke.

The faith also of Jesus' mother, Mary, and her readiness to accept the will of God for her life, regardless of the trouble it may bring, that is credited to her as virtue is contrasted to the reaction of her cousins' husband, priest Zacharias, who on receiving God's messenger proceeded to question the validity of the statements made by his heavenly visitor! Mary's response is recorded as:

Luke 1: 38
New International Version (NIV)

"I am the Lord's servant," Mary answered. "May your word to me be fulfilled." Then the angel left her.

Throughout Jesus' life he honoured his mother making provision for her while nailed to the cross he entrusts her care to the disciple John:

John 19: 26-27
New International Version (NIV)

When Jesus saw his mother there, and the disciple whom he loved standing nearby, he said to her, "Woman, here is your son," and to the disciple, "Here is your mother." From that time on, this disciple took her into his home.

More than likely it's due to the impoverished position of women in the society of the time that Jesus' attitudes towards women, which were in stark contrast to the Jews, were clearly so welcomed. No doubt this is why so many of these encounters are recorded in the Gospels and why he received so many women followers.

Jesus' feminine revolution continued after his ascension and is attested to in the number of female disciples who receive greetings in the letters of the early church that make up the epistles. These same Epistles however again contain some difficult verses to reconcile with a loving God who doesn't discriminate between the sexes. Understood correctly, what these verses are establishing is the best use of the differing qualities possessed by men and women in the sphere of Church life. One of the qualities man is credited with, as exemplified by the Eden scenario, is being better suited to being the leader rather than the follower when it comes to spiritual decisions. That's not to say man is better, or that God loves men more than women anymore than he loves the wealthy more than poor –

Galatians 3: 26-28
New International Version (NIV)

So in Christ Jesus you are all children of God through faith, for all of you who were baptized into Christ have clothed yourselves with Christ. There is neither Jew nor Gentile, neither slave nor free, nor is there male and female, for you are all one in Christ Jesus.

but rather that there are different gifts given to each sex, which although means there is a need to differentiate between the sexes in Church employment, does not make man independent of woman or woman separate from man. For neither would exist without the other!

1 Corinthians 11: 11-12
New International Version (NIV)

Nevertheless, in the Lord woman is not independent of man, nor is man independent of woman. For as woman came from man, so also man is born of woman. But everything comes from God.

The same theme can be gleamed from other initially perplexing verses where Paul seems to lay down some rather strange draconian regulation with regards to women's dress in church, insisting that women cover their heads! The manner of the language, to be honest, I still find is a little abrasive, yet considering Paul's previous employment as Christian hunter and supervisor of stoning's, this may not be surprising.

Although insistence on wearing a head scarf in church would, here and now, seem a humiliating restriction to place upon a woman, these scriptures ought not to be taken out of their context which is the culture of worship in that specific place and time. The Message Bible translation conveys it well:

1 Corinthians 11: 10-16
The Message (MSG)

Don't, by the way, read too much into the differences here between men and women. Neither man nor woman can go it alone or claim priority. Man was created first, as a beautiful shining reflection of God—that is true. But the head on a woman's body clearly outshines in beauty the head of her "head," her husband. The first woman came from man, true—but ever since then, every man comes from a woman! And since virtually everything comes from God anyway, let's quit going through these "who's first" routines.

Don't you agree there is something naturally powerful in the symbolism—a woman, her beautiful hair reminiscent of angels, praying in adoration; a man, his head bared in reverence, praying in submission? I hope you're not going to be argumentative about this. All God's churches see it this way; I don't want you standing out as an exception.

The covering of the hair then, in that time and place, was seen as a symbolic gesture of laying aside your crown before God the same as removing a hat would be a sign of respect for a man.

Alarm bells may be ringing when we hear the husband described as the "head" until we understand that Jesus taught that to serve in this life was to rule in the next, this is why he washed his Disciple's feet, an act which was traditionally reserved for the lowest of the low in the household. In a Christian marriage, with ideally the man and woman seeking only to serve one another as best they could, with the man giving his all for his wife, to be the head is as much a role of service as it is leadership.

To try a put the lid on this now, the work of reformation in the human heart today is no longer a written law but a work of the heart wrought through the Holy Spirit as he now guides those who have accepted him. The influence of which, I would argue, has been the catalyst to the rapid advancement of social order that has made the very subject of equality such a hot topic. Should we require supporting evidence of this then try examining the social norms of the societies that have no Christian heritage and you will find the offensive, discriminatory practises of the "ancient world" alive and well. Although the world God started with sounds pretty ugly to us now, the very fact that it does, particularly here in this nation founded on the teachings of His son, stands only as a testimony to the great work He has already done.

The clearest example to us that God does not discriminate between male and female is the repeated examples of women in the New Testament being filled with the Holy Spirit the very person of God, in the upper room at Pentecost and memorably in the account of the meeting between Elizabeth and Mary, the mother of Jesus.

Luke 1: 39-55
New International Version (NIV)

At that time Mary got ready and hurried to a town in the hillcountry of Judea, where she entered Zechariah's home and greeted Elizabeth. When Elizabeth heard Mary's greeting, the baby leaped in her womb, and Elizabeth was filled with the Holy Spirit. In a loud voice she exclaimed: "Blessed are you among women, and blessed is the child you will bear! But why am I so favoured, that the mother of my Lord should come to me? As soon as the sound of your greeting reached my ears, the baby in my womb leaped for joy. Blessed is she who has believed that the Lord would fulfill his promises to her!"

And Mary said:

"My soul glorifies the Lord
* and my spirit rejoices in God my Saviour,*
* for he has been mindful*
* of the humble state of his servant.*
From now on all generations will call me blessed,
* for the Mighty One has done great things for me—*
* holy is his name.*
His mercy extends to those who fear him,
* from generation to generation.*
He has performed mighty deeds with his arm;
* he has scattered those who are proud in their inmost thoughts.*
He has brought down rulers from their thrones
* but has lifted up the humble.*
He has filled the hungry with good things
* but has sent the rich away empty.*
He has helped his servant Israel,
* remembering to be merciful*
to Abraham and his descendants forever,
* just as he promised our ancestors."*

OH NO NOT JESUS

WOMEN AND THE BIBLE

Women have, and always will be, central to the purposes of God; they were pivotal in the early Church and seeing as the Church tends to be female in majority, it's safe to say, that is still that case and that the message that Jesus loves without discrimination based upon gender is coming through loud and clear through the

Holy Spirit in our age.

Jesus Today and Forever

There were originally, in my plan, a couple of chapters beyond here but I feel at this point we have covered, in reasonable depth, most of the major intellectual obstacles that I wrestled with, in the first year or so, after coming to faith and the other bits I think I should be able to cram into here without it being detrimental the book as a whole.

I hope that the preceding chapters have been helpful in counter-acting at least some of the popular myths and misconceptions about the teachings of Jesus. If there is anything you feel I might have missed or not expounded upon in sufficient depth then please let me know. To briefly recap on the previous chapters:

In "Encounters of a Holy Kind" I shared with you my own testimony of how I came to faith in Jesus Christ and how these experiences tie in with the teachings of the Bible. My hope being that in sharing these experiences you, you would be bold enough to commit some time to seeking out God for yourself.

In "Adam and Eve: You Don't Expect Me to Believe That", I asked that we try to forget our ill-gotten pre-conceptions about this much maligned biblical opener temporarily as we look afresh at the culture-shaping and life-affirming message that the Creation narrative provides, with regards to the dynamics of the relationship between mankind, the created world and our role within it. Subsequently, we tackled a major stumbling block of the message of the Bible for many, obviously including myself, in the unnervingly accurate assessment of our hearts' inclination towards its creator. We then went on to show how even here the Gospel makes an appearance.

The next chapter "The Devil, Hell and All That Scary Stuff" dealt with a subject which, coming from my background of oneness and eastern thinking, was perhaps the biggest for me. Here, I lay before you the scenario that if we are to ever believe that God and the created world truly possess the characteristics attributed to them in the biblical view of our formation, then there must be an alternative explanation for the evil that we see at work in the world. I then went on to describe some of the character traits of this entity as I have come to understand them. Although this teaching is the last thing anyone would want to accept as truth, and as much as we need not dwell too much on such matters, we equally live in ignorance of such things at our own peril, particularly if we have made a decision to seek out Jesus in a spiritual environment that is hostile towards Him and those counted as His.

The forth chapter dealt with reconciling the world's ills with the assurance that God is "A Loving God" who is personally involved with His creation. Understanding the world as strictly man's domain where he has complete autonomy, and bearing in mind God's assessment of our collective and wilful corruption, to blame God for the world's ills only further serves to reinforce the timeless truths of the Eden narrative where Adam blames God for his own failings. Yet for our creator's part, we know from the prophetic words of Jesus himself that God is due to call an end to suffering sometime soon, yet remembering that his perspective is eternal and the bounds of His knowledge are limitless, we must trust in His judgement with regards to the appropriate time for His appearing.

The fifth chapter dealt with the "Authenticity of the Bible" and gave historical reasons as to why there is reason to believe that the writings that comprise the Bible we read today are authentic. We also touched on the subject of prophecy which goes some way to lending practical credence to the claim that these writings have, at their heart, a supernatural source.

We took a look at the Bibles attitudes towards sex in the sixth chapter, where I tried to convey that the attitudes of the Bible towards sex, have first a spiritual dimension, in that we are created to be led by the spirit of God and not the desires of our temporary physical frame and second, a practical dimension in that, without being prudish or prickly, the traditional family life beats any alternative hands down when all is said and done.

In the seventh chapter, "So Someone Died 2000 Years Ago on a Cross...", I attempted to provide an insight into the "how" of the Cross by presenting to you the repeated foretelling of the eternal, spiritual work that was wrought in the Cross over 2000 years ago that is available to us today when we seek God through His son Jesus Christ.

The eighth chapter looked at what bearing the horrific actions of individuals who profess to adhere to the teachings of Jesus Christ, and similarly religious institutions, have on the validity of our enquiry into the substance of the Gospel. Predictably, we are confronted once again with the failings of mankind to fulfil his responsibilities as God's earthly representative, a weakness that wasn't shared by the one in whom we are able to put our full trust, Jesus Christ. After all, it is He who is "the author and finisher of our faith" not He who is the author and the Church of England or the Roman Catholic Church that is the finisher!

Finally, we needed to understand the culture of the times to show that far from devaluing women, Jesus actually brought about a revolution in His time with regards to the role of women within society, a process that has continued to this day, but is predictably absent from cultures that have no foundation in His teachings.

Ultimately, the overcoming of these obstacles were part of the process of bringing my thoughts into line with what I already knew in my heart: that Jesus was the Son of God, that it was He alone who held the keys to living a life in this world whilst having heaven living within our hearts. My major concern about this project is that by expounding on these subjects in the practical, matter of fact way I have, I will have done a disservice to you with regards to communicating the overwhelming joy and daily adventure of walking this life with Jesus as your Guide, Lord, Saviour, best friend and so much more.

I hope that, at least in some small way, reading these chapters has brought you closer to Jesus. I would fully expect that you may at some point question whether my own motives are entirely wholesome, so in answer to that: clearly I was never going to win any popularity contest among my former peers with this, neither is Christian apologetics a particularly hot topic in the publishing world at the moment, but for the record this writing has been a fulfilment of a burden placed on my heart by God in the prayer room, particularly for the people I grew up with and the friends I have met since anyone else I can get to read it is a bonus.

Whether or not you accept my arguments about who Jesus is this will of course be ultimately dependent on our perception of Him alone, which as I asserted in the opening chapter is a truth which can only be revealed by God.

John 3: 1-3
New International Version (NIV)

Now there was a Pharisee, a man named Nicodemus who was a member of the Jewish ruling council. He came to Jesus at night and said, "Rabbi, we know that you are a teacher who has come from God. For no one could perform the signs you are doing if God were not with him." Jesus replied, "Very truly I tell you, no one can see the kingdom of God unless they are born again."

The preceding scripture re-emphasises the importance that seeking, finding and then making the decision to accept God's word has on our perception of His teaching. Nicodemus no doubt was expecting that Jesus would be pleasantly refreshed to hear a member of the notorious ruling Pharisees confirming the validity of His ministry, yet instead of thanks, for his daring declaration of support for Jesus, Nicodemus received correction from the Lord who states plainly that if he is not "born again" by the spirit of God he is unable to perceive what is of God and what is not.

Nevertheless, we must accept that this teaching is a peculiar thing to profess belief in, and the further society distances itself from it, the more peculiar the Gospel sounds:

To stand as a witness to the fact that by virtue of God's grace (unmerited favour) we have come to know and gratefully confess our wholehearted belief that just over 2000 years ago a man walked this earth who was no ordinary man, but the son of the only real God, the creator of our entire physical reality; to accept the Gospel as a message of love from God and Jesus as His gift to all mankind, that through Him we may be forgiven of God, for our mistrust and rebellion and granted renewed joy in this life and everlasting life, in the joy of His presence, in the next; to acknowledge our belief that it is for this reason that on that Friday all those years ago He suffered the Cross and then on the third day following He arose to life to bear witness of this work and to accept that following this He ascended into heaven where He will remain until His self-prophesied return to the earth is either the most wondrous thing ever or sheer nonsense, even on chapter 10.

Yet as nonsensical as it sounds to Man, we need to be mindful again of our own fallibility. Between the lines of the parables of Jesus, we read the message that "things are not always what they seem" and as our culture continues to give no credence to the Gospel, we might try considering the possibility that as technologically superior as we are to our predecessors, it doesn't automatically follow that our perception of the nature of reality is equally as advanced.

I know I am repeating myself here but there is, after all, surely hope and a valid testimony of itself in the fact that man, who has managed to fulfil the prediction of the 19th century German philosopher Friedrich Nietzsche in making the 20th century the bloodiest yet, finds this once revered Gospel, that has been so fundamental in the formation of the most successful democracies in our world, jarring against his spirit again; prompting his rapid rejection of its message.

In my youth, when I was attempting to somehow bottle the

remaining dregs of the joy and vibrant innocence of my youth into a piece of music, I never considered that what I desired might be found in Jesus Christ. When I was even younger and I would gaze with a deep longing in my heart out of the window, on the little landing of our house in Woodsetts, across open summer fields to the horizon, never would I have thought that the source and the fulfilment of that longing would be this. He is the never-drying fountain of life that once flowed in our hearts, that made summers seem never-ending, that made autumn wondrous, winter exciting and spring refreshing. It is He who puts the life in life and without whom life gradually, yet inevitably, becomes considerably less.

Reality is this: that the world with all its pressing concerns and busyness will soon no longer be our concern and behind it all always stands Jesus. On some level, as I stated in the opening chapter, I always knew this, yet on encountering Him this was merely amplified. He is the great revealer of truth. In a cynical world, where I could be the worst of cynics, that counts all things as worthless, He is worthy. Worthy of there being limits to our cynicism and boundaries to our jokes; worthy of honouring and acknowledging Him as truth, goodness and light in a dark world. Jesus meek and mild, adored by the faithful, the King of Kings born in lowliness, who lived to serve and is now exalted to the right-hand (the position of power and influence) of God, continually calling out to Man that Man may heed His voice and let Him in to save Man from himself and the consequences of his own folly.

As a grateful recipient of His saving grace, it is to Him now that has given so much that I offer that even more unfashionable and peculiar commodity: my worship. Worship in the sense not only of a celebration on a Sunday but that He now, before all else, is my aim, direction and the wind in my sails, rather than any self-centred concern which may have consumed my energies in the past. Because His love has so overwhelmed my fears and the light of His presence so enlightened the darkest corners of my heart that my desire is simply to give Him all and anything I can in expression of my gratitude. I can relate now to the words of "In the Bleak Mid-Winter" that formed part of the Queen's Christmas message the year just gone:

What can I give Him, Poor as I am?
If I were a shepherd. I would bring a lamb,
If I were a wise man. I would do my part,
Yet what I can I give Him, Give my heart.

Because over and over again He has proved Himself trustworthy, I am left with no reason to doubt His goodness or His faithfulness to His word that "no one will snatch me from his hand".

John 10: 24-28
New International Version (NIV)

The Jews who were there gathered around him, saying, "How long will you keep us in suspense? If you are the Messiah, tell us plainly."

Jesus answered, "I did tell you, but you do not believe. The works I do in my Father's name testify about me, but you do not believe because you are not my sheep. My sheep listen to my voice; I know them, and they follow me. I give them eternal life, and they shall never perish; no one will snatch them out of my hand."

Salvation

The motive all of this of course being love: "For God so loved the world..." Not because God needs Man but because Man without God is lost. Some of these chapters will no doubt have been hard work, the issues they address were certainly hard work for me to overcome anyway, yet when you are personally involved with someone then you tell them the uncomfortable truths. God loves us, so He doesn't mind upsetting us if it's a truth we need to hear.

This act of giving though, that God has initiated, is one that necessitates a response to which there are only two responses: rejection or acceptance. Deferment is simply rejection until further notice. We often believe that the ultimate question to be answered in life is "does God Love us?", yet because this question has been answered so emphatically in Jesus, the true pivotal question of life now is "do we love God?" and it is ours to answer.

The question then is: if we choose to accept the message of the Gospel, what is required of us?

I have placed great emphasis through these discourses on seeking an encounter with the living Christ and I know already that some of those reading this have experienced their own revelation. As life changing as these experiences are, however, they do not alone constitute accepting Jesus and salvation. They are but a call to it.

As some of the very earliest doubts that arose after accepting Jesus were with regards to whether I had done all that was necessary, to ensure that we are not deceived let me outline from scripture how we go about accept the gift of God. Fortunately, having done all the hard work Himself, our part is made very simple by Jesus.

Luke 23: 32-43
New International Version (NIV)

Two other men, both criminals, were also led out with him to be executed. When they came to the place called the Skull, they crucified him there, along with the criminals—one on his right, the other on his left. Jesus said, "Father, forgive them, for they do not know what they are doing." And they divided up his clothes by casting lots. The people stood watching, and the rulers even sneered at him. They said, "He saved others; let him save himself if he is God's Messiah, the Chosen One." The soldiers also came up and mocked him. They offered him wine vinegar and said, "If you are the king of the Jews, save yourself." There was a written notice above him, which read: this is the king of the jews. One of the criminals who hung there hurled insults at him: "Aren't you the

Messiah? Save yourself and us!" But the other criminal rebuked him. "Don't you fear God," he said, "since you are under the same sentence? We are punished justly, for we are getting what our deeds deserve. But this man has done nothing wrong." Then he said, "Jesus, remember me when you come into your kingdom." Jesus answered him, "Truly I tell you, today you will be with me in paradise."

In the scripture above there are several important confessions that the second thief makes that provide an insight into his heart as he seeks salvation that can guide us:

Firstly, he acknowledges God as the ruling authority over creation and himself.

Secondly, he admits his guilt, also acknowledging that he has received from life his due, that it is him and not God who is responsible for his forlorn state. (He is no longer accusing God as was the case in the Garden.)

He acknowledges the righteousness of Jesus Christ.

Finally, knowing he is lost without a saviour, he requests from Jesus salvation, yet his humility is apparent in that he merely asks if Jesus would "remember him"; in contrast to the other thief who demanded that he prove his kingship with immediate effect, this man is humbly and openly acknowledging the Son of God who came from Glory.

Jesus sees the desire of his heart and saves him.

If we have arrived at the same truth as this man, if we have come to the realisation that to go any further through life's journey with ourselves as our only guide would be fruitless. If we have a penitent,repentant heart with regards to our own actions from which our lost-ness has become our reward then all that is required of us is that we simply acknowledge and confess the truth of these things before God in prayer and ask Him, in the name of Jesus Christ His son, to save us.

(If needed, there is a prayer to follow on a separate page at the end of this chapter.)

Then, no matter where you may be or what the situation or when or how the truth of who He is was revealed to you from heaven, be it a host of angels in the clouds or a strange sensation at the mention of His name, today salvation is yours.

1 John 1: 8-9
New International Version (NIV)

If we claim to be without sin, we deceive ourselves and the truth is not in us. If we confess our sins, he is faithful and just and will forgive us our sins and purify us from all unrighteousness.

Again, as with other scriptures, here the translation could be better. What John is saying is that if we agree with God about His assessment of our rebellion then He will cleanse our conscience and restore us to our pre-fallen state.

Accepting Jesus as our Lord and Saviour is no small thing at all. It is, in the words of Jesus, crossing over "from death to life", it is what He described to the Jewish teacher, Nicodemus, as being born again.

If, on the other hand, we do not consider ourselves as falling into the category of requiring salvation then I would implore you to heed the stark disclosure that follows John's recourse on salvation quoted above:

1 John 1: 10
New International Version (NIV)

If we claim we have not sinned, we make him out to be a liar and his word is not in us.

In the book of Isaiah, the word of God declares that throughout the annals of time, from the beginning of this age to the end, we have all like sheep gone astray, each of us preferring and pursuing our own ideas of God, rather than the truth.

Isaiah 53: 6
New International Version (NIV)

We all, like sheep, have gone astray,
  each of us has turned to our own way;
and the Lord has laid on him
  the iniquity of us all.

God has named the sickness and provided the cure, the question of our life is do we want it?

Why was I so opposed to the teachings of Jesus more than any other? Simply because without knowing much about it I still knew that as far as my life was concerned I didn't measure up to the standards of living outlined by Jesus in the Bible. So often the last thing we want to do is have it confirmed by reading about it. But Jesus, aware that this would be the case, said specifically that He did not come to condemn the world but to save it.

Our only issue following understanding this is that we don't like being told when we're wrong. Even though really often we know we're wrong, and even though God has unlocked the door to our restoration and reconciliation to Him, we still refuse to agree with God about our situation. God loves us but He doesn't love everything we do or our attitude towards Him.

What we'd prefer though is a God that will agree with us and call good what we want to call good, and call bad what we call bad. The consequence of this attitude is that we call the God that displays his infinite love in the Cross, with nails through his hands and feet, unloving because he doesn't tow our party line!

God is not us and He knows we have fallen short of our calling, but He is just waiting for us to cast our glance towards Him and away from ourselves that He may reveal to us His overwhelming grace and His limitless love.

Song of Solomon 4: 9
Common English Bible (CEB)

You have captured my heart, my sister, my bride!
You have captured my heart with one glance from your eyes,

The bride in the scripture above being a metaphor for those called out of the world, i.e. the Church in its original sense.

Going Forward

Just before I wrap this thing up for good, I wanted to leave a brief overview that may not be of utmost importance immediately, but will at least be here to refer to later when the subjects addressed come into view in should you have decide to embark on a walk of faith.

If we have prayed the salvation prayer then we truly have crossed over from death to life and, as such, living things will need feeding. A bare minimum to do is to get ourselves a Bible and start reading it. Be encouraged when the words that were once cold are now brought alive by the deposit of God's spirit within you. This is your spiritual food now. The Gospel of John is probably the most cohesive and readable book of the Bible, or most akin to a novel, and often recommended as a starting point for newcomers, followed by the other Gospels and the book of Acts, the "what the disciples did next" book.

It would also be of benefit to us, whilst heeding the direction of the Holy Spirit, to find a good active, hopefully vibrant, Church. The thing not to do is to seek answers from those who do not know Jesus and have never walked the path you are now walking. It's simply not common sense. So find a good Church that has Bible study or nurturing classes, or anything where you get to ask questions basically and join in.

This all may sound like a bit too much of a culture shock for some, however the Bible tells us that "the children perish though lack of knowledge" and after the initial rush of joy of finding our saviour there is no trophy our old foe would like more than one of God's own redeemed falling for his deception a second time...

So if we can find some faithful believers that can encourage us and answer any fears we may have then there are obvious benefits in terms of growing in our new life. We must bear in mind however that Church organisations are run by humans and therefore are never perfect and that all sound teaching ought to be accompanied by the testimony of the Holy Spirit bearing witness to the truth of it.

Isaiah 54: 4-13
New International Version (NIV)

"Do not be afraid; you will not be put to shame.
  Do not fear disgrace; you will not be humiliated.
You will forget the shame of your youth
  and remember no more the reproach of your widowhood.

 For your Maker is your husband—
   the Lord Almighty is his name—
the Holy One of Israel is your Redeemer;
  he is called the God of all the earth.

 The Lord will call you back
   as if you were a wife deserted and distressed in spirit—
a wife who married young,
   only to be rejected," says your God.
For a brief moment I abandoned you,
  but with deep compassion I will bring you back.

In a surge of anger
 I hid my face from you for a moment,
but with everlasting kindness
 I will have compassion on you,"
 says the Lord your Redeemer.

"To me this is like the days of Noah,
 when I swore that the waters of Noah would never again cover
the earth.
So now I have sworn not to be angry with you,
 never to rebuke you again.
 Though the mountains be shaken
 and the hills be removed,
yet my unfailing love for you will not be shaken
 nor my covenant of peace be removed,"
 says the Lord, who has compassion on you.

"Afflicted city, lashed by storms and not comforted,
 I will rebuild you with stones of turquoise,
 your foundations with lapis lazuli.
I will make your battlements of rubies,
 your gates of sparkling jewels,
 and all your walls of precious stones.
All your children will be taught by the Lord,
 and great will be their peace."

Let me not mislead you in a further matter though, that intellectual obstacles are not the only obstacles to be faced along the road of faith. When Jesus said he was the way, he meant it literally in that to some degree we will inevitably share in his experiences of spiritual opposition which can often manifest by those closest to us.

Matthew 16: 23
New International Version (NIV)

Jesus turned and said to Peter, "Get behind me, Satan! You are a stumbling block to me; you do not have in mind the concerns of God, but merely human concerns."

We may experience rejection from those who have always been welcoming and find that, when the tyre hits the road in standing for the truth, we are alone. Suffice to say, should it appear as though all hell is breaking loose in your life for no particular reason then be assured that you are drawing near to God and more than likely a deeper understanding and revelation of God is around the next corner.

The first year of our Christian lives, once the dust has settled on our initial salvation, may be the most difficult. Jesus tells us that once an unclean spirit has left a person, it roams around, gathers some friends and returns to where it came from. If this is the case, as I have found, then let's not hesitate in drawing as close to God as possible from the off. Then when the accuser returns, Jesus is waiting! Getting close to Him through prayer and study of the word early on and experiencing the joy found in His presence will ensure that when anything not of God appears in our spirit, it will be so at odds with the holy fire burning within us that its source will be instantly recognisable and a quick swift to the rear in Jesus' name will be all that is required. Or, as a visiting lady preacher to church put it, that whenever Satan comes knocking at the door she sends Jesus to answer it! We would do well to follow her advice if we are to make it through our early Christian life to become the "good soil" in The Parable of the Sower:

Matthew 13: 3-9
New International Version (NIV)

Then he told them many things in parables, saying: "A farmer went out to sow his seed. As he was scattering the seed, some fell along the path, and the birds came and ate it up. Some fell on rocky places, where it did not have much soil. It sprang up quickly, because the soil was shallow. But when the sun came up, the plants were scorched, and they withered because they had no root. Other seed fell among thorns, which grew up and choked the plants. Still other seed fell on good soil, where it produced a crop—a hundred, sixty or thirty times what was sown. Whoever has ears, let them hear."

Matthew 13: 18-23
New International Version (NIV)

"Listen then to what the parable of the sower means: When anyone hears the message about the kingdom and does not understand it, the evil one comes and snatches away what was sown in their heart. This is the seed sown along the path. The seed falling on rocky ground refers to someone who hears the word and at once receives it with joy. But since they have no root, they last only a short time. When trouble or persecution comes because of the word, they quickly fall away. The seed falling among the thorns refers to someone who hears the word, but the worries of this life and the deceitfulness of wealth choke the word, making it unfruitful. But the seed falling on good soil refers to someone who hears the word and understands it. This is the one who produces a crop, yielding a hundred, sixty or thirty times what was sown

Baptism

This is a frightening thought to someone who may have only prayed the salvation prayer five minutes previous, but for future references and so that you understand, I thought I would just try and demystify what Baptism is about. Water Baptism is a public declaration of us coming into agreement with God and an outward sign of the inward work that Jesus has done in us. It is the point at which we publicly put all our eggs in one basket, so to speak, and come clean with our peers about the reason for the change within our heart. We hear of how important this was to the early believers who, having taken this step, were able to stick with Jesus when the going got tough, whereas the hardened hearts of the Scribes and the Pharisees simply returned to their old life.

It is clear from the scriptural example of the thief that water Baptism is not a prerequisite for entrance through the pearly gates, yet if we are convinced and wholeheartedly following Jesus in the literal sense then it is a natural and important step for us to take when we are ready. Far from what the world would have you believe, Jesus only requested us to continue to observe a handful of things, Baptism however is one.

The Holy Spirit

Yet this is not the only Baptism mentioned in the Bible. John the Baptist himself talked of a greater Baptism and a greater baptiser than himself.

Matthew 3: 11-12
New International Version (NIV)

"I baptize you with water for repentance. But after me comes one who is more powerful than I, whose sandals I am not worthy to carry. He will baptize you with the Holy Spirit and fire. His winnowing fork is in his hand, and he will clear his threshing floor, gathering his wheat into the barn and burning up the chaff with unquenchable fire."

Although views on the role and the importance of this second Baptism differ between denominations, it is difficult to understand, when taking all the scriptural references to it into account, how the importance of this second working of God's grace was overlooked for centuries until relatively recently. It is clear from John the Baptist and Jesus that throughout the age of the early Church, recorded in the epistles, that the Baptism of the Holy Spirit was a pillar of the Gospel, empowering believers to do exploits for God from its first appearance at the birth of the Church (Pentecost) onwards.

Now whole books have been written on this subject and I don't want to digress too far but I think it's necessary and worthwhile, just to clear up some common misconceptions on the subject of the person of the Holy Spirit:

The Holy Spirit is the current incumbent of the role of Jesus in the world. Once we accept the salvation made available by Jesus, the Holy Spirit dwells within us from that moment onwards as our guide, counsellor and comforter. Yet life is not static, and Jesus talks of a well becoming a spring that becomes a fountain welling up to eternal life; he explains that the life in the Spirit is a life of increase and ever more abundant spiritual blessing. The Baptism of the Holy Spirit is merely a staging post along this journey. It is the gift of God to enable us to choose to allow our Spirit the use of our tongues through the blessing of a prayer language, to live a closer more effective life for His kingdom.

Some people are Baptised immediately, for others it comes years after salvation. Yet for all of us it is something we ought to seek and if we seek, then we have the promise from scripture that we will receive. We may not receive immediately what we asked for, but we will receive what we need to be able to never return with the same question and move forward.

As with all aspects of God's kingdom, the Baptism of the Holy Ghost is voluntary, it is something we seek and choose to be a part of. Speaking in tongues, once blessed with the gift, is a voluntary act of worship, not a voodoo trance. Neither is it the be all and end all, or to be used as badge of holiness.

The badge of holiness we are to wear is our love for one another that the world may see and enquire, not our incomprehensible words. Our gift of tongues is for us personally to bless God with and as we bless we will also receive, yet without love for one another our spiritual gifts are meaningless as the mission of God is to rescue his children, yet if we claim to have fellowship with God yet do not have love for others then what testimony are we giving of God and of our tongues, or whatever other gift we may receive from on high?

John 13: 34-35
New International Version (NIV)

"A new command I give you: Love one another. As I have loved you, so you must love one another. By this everyone will know that you are my disciples, if you love one another."

Salvation Prayer

Eternal and everlasting Father, thank you Lord for speaking to my heart, even though I have rejected you and I have counted you as not worthy of my time or attention, I come to you today because I realise that I am lost. I don't know where I came from or where I am going to, and the more I try the more lost I end up. Jesus, Son of God, please hear my prayer and forgive my sin that I acknowledge before you today. Please save me, guide me and protect me from this day forward and all the days of my life.

Lord of all, hear my prayer in the name of your son Jesus Christ,

Amen

Printed in Great
Britain
by Amazon

31968650R00124